The Shakespeare Handbooks: Shakespeare's Contemporaries
Series Editors: Paul Edmondson & Kevin Ewert

*'Tis Pity She's a Whore* by John Ford is one of the most controversial plays ever staged in the English theatre. In this illuminating Handbook, Martin White:

- offers an in-depth, moment-by-moment analysis of the play, looking at how it might be performed on stage
- provides vital contextual material on Ford's social and literary influences
- reconstructs the play's performances in Ford's own time and examines later stage, television and film productions
- guides the reader through the often heated critical and theatrical responses to the dramatic work.

**Martin White** is Professor of Theatre at the University of Bristol. He has published widely on early modern theatre, directed numerous plays, and has worked as an advisor to the Globe reconstruction in London, and to the RSC.

**The Shakespeare Handbooks** are student-friendly introductory guides which offer a new approach to understanding the plays of Shakespeare and his contemporaries in performance. The commentary at the heart of each volume explores the play's theatrical potential, providing an experience as close as possible to seeing it in the theatre. Ideal for students and teachers of Literature and Theatre, as well as actors and directors, the overall aim is to help a reader reach an independent and well-informed view of each play by imagining how it might be rehearsed or performed on stage.

THE SHAKESPEARE HANDBOOKS

Series Editors: Paul Edmondson and Kevin Ewert
(Founding Series Editor: John Russell Brown)


PUBLISHED

| | |
|---|---|
| John Russell Brown | *Hamlet* |
| John Russell Brown | *Macbeth* |
| John Russell Brown | *King Lear* |
| David Carnegie | *Julius Caesar* |
| Paul Edmondson | *Twelfth Night* |
| Bridget Escolme | *Antony and Cleopatra* |
| Kevin Ewert | *Henry V* |
| Alison Findlay | *Much Ado about Nothing* |
| Trevor R. Griffiths | *The Tempest* |
| Stuart Hampton-Reeves | *Measure for Measure* |
| Stuart Hampton-Reeves | *Othello* |
| Margaret Jane Kidnie | *The Taming of the Shrew* |
| Ros King | *The Winter's Tale* |
| James N. Loehlin | *Henry IV, Parts I and II* |
| Jeremy Lopez | *Richard II* |
| Edward L. Rocklin | *Romeo and Juliet* |
| Lesley Wade Soule | *As You Like It* |
| Martin White | *A Midsummer Night's Dream* |

SHAKESPEARE'S CONTEMPORARIES

| | |
|---|---|
| Jay O'Berski | Middleton and Rowley: *The Changeling* |
| Stephen Purcell | Webster: *The White Devil* |
| Martin White | Ford: *'Tis Pity She's a Whore* |

Other titles are currently in preparation

The Shakespeare Handbooks:
*Shakespeare's Contemporaries*

# John Ford
# 'Tis Pity She's a Whore

Martin White

palgrave
macmillan

First published 2012 by
PALGRAVE MACMILLAN

Palgrave Macmillan in the UK is an imprint of Macmillan Publishers Limited, registered in England, company number 785998, of Houndmills, Basingstoke, Hampshire RG21 6XS.

Palgrave Macmillan in the US is a division of St Martin's Press LLC, 175 Fifth Avenue, New York, NY 10010.

Palgrave Macmillan is the global academic imprint of the above companies and has companies and representatives throughout the world.

Palgrave® and Macmillan® are registered trademarks in the United States, the United Kingdom, Europe and other countries.

ISBN-13: 978–0–230–24298–2 hardback
ISBN-13: 978–0–230–24299–9 paperback

This book is printed on paper suitable for recycling and made from fully managed and sustained forest sources. Logging, pulping and manufacturing processes are expected to conform to the environmental regulations of the country of origin.

A catalogue record for this book is available from the British Library.

A catalog record for this book is available from the Library of Congress.

10  9  8  7  6  5  4  3  2  1
21 20 19 18 17 16 15 14 13 12

Printed in China

*For all my students in Manchester and Bristol whose enthusiasm
over the past forty years for plays such as this has ensured
my own never dimmed*

# Contents

# Series Editors' Preface

The Shakespeare Handbooks provide an innovative way of studying the plays of Shakespeare and his contemporaries in performance. The commentaries, which are their core feature, enable a reader to envisage the words of a text unfurling in performance, involving actions and meanings not readily perceived except in rehearsal or performance. The aim is to present the plays in the environment for which they were written and to offer an experience as close as possible to an audience's progressive experience of a production.

While each book has the same range of contents, their authors have been encouraged to shape them according to their own critical and scholarly understanding and their first-hand experience of theatre practice. The various chapters are designed to complement the commentaries: the cultural context of each play is presented together with quotations from original sources; the authority of its text or texts is considered with what is known of the earliest performances; key performances and productions of its subsequent stage history are both described and compared; an account is given of influential criticism of the play and the more significant is quoted extensively. The aim in all this has been to help readers to develop their own informed and imaginative view of a play in ways that supplement the provision of standard editions and are more user-friendly than detailed stage histories or collections of criticism from diverse sources.

We would like to acknowledge a special debt of gratitude to the founder of the Shakespeare Handbooks Series, John Russell Brown, whose energy for life, literature and theatre we continue to find truly inspiring.

Paul Edmondson and Kevin Ewert

# Preface and Acknowledgements

I have been fortunate to have directed a number of Ford's plays in the Drama Department at the University of Bristol: a workshop production and several practical exercises around 'Tis Pity, a candlelit production of Love's Sacrifice in 1997 on a reconstructed stage and auditorium based on the drawings of an unknown playhouse held in the library at Worcester College, Oxford (see p. 5) and a full production of The Broken Heart which opened the Department's second theatre in 1999. These productions were all created with my students, and I thank them not only for the sheer enjoyment of making these plays together, but also for the opportunities they provided to understand Ford in the best place possible – the rehearsal room. They were also made with my great friend Jennie Norman, who has designed almost every play I have directed since she joined the Department in the early 1980s. The production of Love's Sacrifice was particularly influential in developing my ideas for The Chamber of Demonstrations (2009), my interactive DVD, filmed on a version of the reconstruction developed by Jennie Norman, that explores and, most importantly, *shows* the flexibility and impact of the artificial lighting of an indoor playhouse and also reveals the significance of the particular relationship between the confined performance space, the proximity of the spectators and the text of Ford's plays. The DVD includes scenes from Love's Sacrifice and 'Tis Pity, and I want to thank here not only the professional actors who worked on those scenes – Michael Brown, Monica Dolan, Jamie Glover, Michael Matus and Hattie McDonald – but also Jenny Tiramani who dressed the performances from the wardrobe at Shakespeare's Globe, and whose keen and expert eyes registered and recorded the particular effects of the candlelight on the fabric of the actors' clothes. Others to whom I know I owe my gratitude include Ron Daniels, Lisa Hopkins, Simon Jones, David Leveaux, Jonathan Munby, Tim Pigott-Smith, Matthew

Warchus, the staff of the Shakespeare Centre, Stratford-upon-Avon, and (as always) my colleagues in the University of Bristol Theatre Collection. To these are added all those on whose scholarship I have built my own discussion, my students' perceptive, awkward and valuable questions in seminars, and those actors whose performances on stage and screen have offered me opportunities to understand the play more fully. I was given a year's leave to complete this and other projects, and I am grateful to the Arts Faculty Research Committee for financial assistance with travel and other expenses incurred in the research for this book.

I owe a particular debt to John Russell Brown, who I have known and admired since he took me on to his pioneering MA in Theatre Studies course at the University of Birmingham in the late 1960s. John is a model of how academic study and practice can inform each other, and is everything one hopes for from a General Editor. The editorial staff at Palgrave Macmillan, especially Sonya Barker and Felicity Noble, have throughout been supportive, and supreme models of patience.

But as always, my greatest thanks are to Alison Steele and our children, Hannah and Nathaniel, for their support not only with this book, but also with everything else I do.

# 1 *The Text and Early Performances*

John Ford was christened in St Michael's Church in his home village of Ilsington, in Devon, on 12 April 1586. His father Thomas was a local landowner, and his mother Elizabeth (née Popham) was a niece of John Popham, a successful lawyer who a year after John's birth presided at the trial of Mary, Queen of Scots and later became Elizabeth I's Lord Chief Justice. In 1600, John's older brother Henry left Devon for London and the Middle Temple, one of the four Inns of Court, where, after a brief period at Exeter College, Oxford, John joined him two years later. Middle Temple was one of the law schools which together made up what Sir Edward Coke described in 1602 as 'the third university', after Oxford and Cambridge. But as well as training those who would make the law their career and educating the sons of the nobility and country gentry, the Inns were also a vibrant centre of literary and dramatic activity. The Hall of Middle Temple (destroyed in the Second World War but fully restored) was the venue for plays and masques, where, for example, on the feast of Candlemas, 2 February 1602, the Lord Chamberlain's Men (Shakespeare's company, with the writer himself probably among the cast) staged *Twelfth Night*.

Next to nothing is known of Ford's activities at Middle Temple, and although references to and borrowings from a wide range of plays, and the use of theatrical metaphors in his early prose and poetry suggest he was a keen theatre-goer, neither the opportunity to see professional performances nor to rub shoulders with up-and-coming dramatists such as John Marston (who was a contemporary) seem to have inspired him at this point in his life to write plays. His earliest published work was *Fame's Memorial* (1606), a verse elegy on the death of the Earl of Devonshire, Lord Mountjoy, dedicated to his widow, Lady Penelope. In 1581, forced to marry Lord Rich, Penelope had nevertheless pursued an open affair with Mountjoy, bearing him five children and, following her divorce from Rich, she had married him in 1605. He died three months later. Ford described the subject of *Fame's Memorial* as 'a theme for every stage', and as a real-life story of 'forced marriage, enduring emotional loyalty and defiance of a hypocritically flexible social morality' (Wymer 1995: 94), it prefigured the themes of many of his plays. He followed this with *Honour Triumphant, or The Peers' Challenge*, a prose pamphlet on the subject of love and beauty, dedicated to the Countesses of Pembroke and Montgomery, and both these early works seem to indicate he was hoping to find an aristocratic patron. Throughout the second decade of the century he continued to write poems – *A Funeral Elegy* (1612), *The Golden Mean* (1613), subtitled 'The Nobleness of perfect virtue in extremes', and *Christ's Bloody Sweat* (1613). This last work was a lengthy, 64-page reflection on Christ's suffering and many of Ford's plays, including *'Tis Pity*, show close verbal parallels with it. He also wrote further prose works, including a biography, now lost, of his former colleague at Middle Temple, Sir Thomas Overbury, murdered in the Tower of London (1615) and *A Line of Life* (1620), which like *'Tis Pity* showed a knowledge of the playwright George Chapman's work. Although not yet a dramatist himself, Ford was evidently mixing with playwrights, producing commendatory verses for Barnabe Barnes' play *Four Books of Office* (1606), Webster's *The Duchess of Malfi* (1614), Shirley's *The Wedding* (1629) and for two plays by Massinger – *The Roman Actor* (1626) and *The Great Duke of Florence* (1638).

Ford's collaboration with Thomas Dekker on *The Witch of Edmonton* (1621) was most likely his first foray into playwriting, and the start of 'a career that was to make him the most original and imaginative playwright of the Caroline period' (Leggatt 1988: 226; 'Caroline', from the Latin 'Carolus', refers to the reign of Charles I). He worked with Dekker (and other collaborators) on at least seven plays before, in 1628, aged 42, he wrote his first independent play, which was probably *The Lover's Melancholy*, a tragicomedy clearly indebted to the discussion of mental illness in Robert Burton's *Anatomy of Melancholy*, which would also be a strong influence on *'Tis Pity* (see p. 102). However, we cannot be sure exactly how many plays he wrote overall, or even whether all those that bear his name are actually his. Those we *can* be certain of are the seven plays, including *The Lover's Melancholy*, published in the years between 1628 and 1639: *The Broken Heart, 'Tis Pity She's a Whore,*

*Love's Sacrifice, Perkin Warbeck, The Fancies, Chaste and Noble* and *The Lady's Trial*. Added to these may be his collaborations with Thomas Dekker, *The Queen*, published anonymously in 1653 but now generally attributed to Ford, and *possibly* some among the seven lost plays with which he is associated in seventeenth-century documents. The date of his death is unknown, though it was probably later than 1639, the year in which *The Lady's Trial* – his last known play – appeared in print and to which he attached a dedicatory epistle.

## Date and text

*'Tis Pity She's a Whore* was published in 1633, printed by Nicholas Okes for Richard Collins, and sold by him at his shop in the churchyard of St Paul's Cathedral, 'at the signe of the three Kings'. Although, given its nature, we might understandably picture the writer of *'Tis Pity* as a rebellious young man, Ford was in fact nearing fifty when the play was first published in 1633. The title page does not name him as the writer, but the epistle dedicated to the Earl of Peterborough, Lord Mordaunt, that precedes the text is signed 'JOHN FORD', though what debt Ford had incurred, or future benefit he hoped for from the Earl, is unknown. The epistle, the commendatory verse by Thomas Ellice (not included in all copies; see p. 133) and the play-text are all set in roman type with some words in emphatic italic type. This mix of type faces is not unique in early modern publishing, but nor is it common, and the fact that it is found consistently in copies of Ford's plays may suggest that the way they appeared in print was of particular interest to him; as Peter Ure observed, if these typographical features were authorial, they would constitute 'an element in the play which is a genuine and irreducible part of the author's conception' (1968: xxi). This apparent care in presentation may also help explain the apology for printing errors inserted at the end of the text, which was possibly written by Ford himself, or at least added by the printer at the playwright's insistence (Massai, 2011).

But while we have a publication date, and a place of performance (Christopher Beeston's Phoenix Playhouse; see below), exactly when the play was written is less easily determined. It was common practice for acting companies – who owned the copyright – to release a play for publication soon after its premiere if it failed to attract an audience or, if had originally been successful, when it ceased to be a box-office draw. Plays were also sold to publishers at times of plague when the playhouses were closed and it was necessary to find ways to replace lost income. We have no evidence of the play's reception when it first appeared on stage, but the fact that it is still listed in the late 1630s among the plays owned by Beeston may suggest it held its value commercially, and it may well have been performed at court on one or more of the 49 occasions Beeston's company, Queen Henrietta's Men, performed at court between 1629 and 1633, as well as on tour.

In trying to establish a date of composition, the dedicatory epistle to Peterborough includes the puzzling phrase 'First Fruits of my leisure' (note the emphatic italics) which has been a source of speculation. The term 'first fruits' usually refers to the first part of a harvest which was sometimes made into an offering to the Church or, more colloquially, to the first profits from any undertaking. If we were to understand the phrase to mean that 'Tis Pity was his first play – or, assuming that it postdates collaborative work such as The Witch of Edmonton, perhaps his first solo play – it would put its composition date earlier than The Lover's Melancholy. However, the expression of a debt to Peterborough might suggest that the earl had given Ford the opportunity to concentrate on this particular play and that 'first fruits' simply refers to the successful outcome of that time, rather than to the launch of his career as a whole. Discussions of its date are also blurred by the 'feel' of the play, which for some critics has a character and spirit more associated with the 1620s than the 1630s; Una Ellis-Fermor, for example, considered Ford to be 'the inheritor of security of the later Jacobean mood' (1965: 227), Clifford Leech saw the play as being different from Ford's other tragedies in that he managed 'to re-create ... the Jacobean tragic spirit' (1957: 49), and J.W. Lever thought it should be taken as the last of the Jacobean tragedies of blood (1971: 11). However, we also need to remember that Ford consciously and productively drew on the work of his predecessors (see p. 89). As a result of these conflicting issues and their varied interpretations a wide range of suggestions for a date of composition has been presented, from the early 1620s to 1633, none of which can be proved conclusively. (See Hopkins 2010: 1–5 for a useful summary of views of the play's date.)

## First performances

When it comes to the place the play was first performed we are on solid ground, as the 1633 title page tells us that the play was 'Acted by the Queenes Maiesties Servants, at The Phoenix in Drury Lane'. This playhouse was the project of Christopher Beeston, converted from a former cock-fighting venue, and although it advertised its location as fashionable Drury Lane, the playhouse was actually tucked away between Drury Lane and Wild Street – where the Peabody Housing Estate now stands – with access via a now-defunct lane, Cockpit Alley. The Queen's Majesty's Servants, or Queen Henrietta's Men as the company was more frequently known (their patron was Charles I's new wife, Henrietta Maria), had been formed by Beeston in 1625, following the eight-month closure of the playhouses during the longest outbreak of plague in London's history which had also been the death of his previous company, the Lady Elizabeth's Men. When he set up business again, a number of actors from that company joined the new venture, including Richard Perkins, one of the most famous actors of his day, along with players from other companies. Indeed, the fact that Perkins, then a member of the eminent King's Men (the only company to survive the closure), was persuaded to join the new company must have been a real boost to the venture's hopes of success. And a success it proved, artistic and commercial, remaining at the playhouse for a further ten years – the only company to stay at the Phoenix for longer than three years.

Ford wrote all his independent plays either for the indoor theatre in Blackfriars, home to the King's Men, or for the Phoenix, and they show how he exploited the resources of the indoor stage to the full, as well as reflecting the particular nature and composition of his audience in his work. In the following section I shall try to reconstruct how some scenes in *'Tis Pity* were designed to take advantage of the Phoenix, while in Chapter 2 I have indicated where the particularly close interdependence between Ford's text and his playhouse raises implications for modern performances. Although we have no visual evidence for the interior of any particular indoor playhouse, we can be reasonably certain of the features they would have shared. They were, of course, roofed, and all the spectators were seated: in the pit, the boxes to the sides of the stage and in the galleries at two levels, with the upper level running across at the rear of the stage, creating, in effect a theatre-in-the-round. The indoor playhouses were by comparison with the outdoor playhouses such as the Globe small: the stage at the Blackfriars, for example, was less than half the size of that at the Globe. (See White 2009 for images of an indoor playhouse similar to the Phoenix.)

Although indoor playhouses are often referred to as 'private', they were in fact no more so than the 'public' outdoor playhouses. But they charged a lot more for admission, with a lowest ticket priced at sixpence, six times what the public playhouses asked for, rising to a massive two shillings and sixpence for a stage box, prices more similar to those for opera tickets today compared with those for theatre. For that enhanced price, however, they did offer a unique theatrical experience for their audiences compared to what was on offer at outdoor playhouses such as the Globe. It was an intimate, even claustrophobic space, where actors and audience were particularly close to each other: a space for conversational delivery and where the physical presence of the actor was even more potent. There were two further defining characteristics of indoor performances: music was employed to a greater degree than outdoors and the stage was lit by candles, with some added daylight from windows, while candles, lanterns and torches carried by actors were used to help set or focus the onstage action. Music was played before the play began, during the intervals and, significantly, during the performance itself. It would have been played on string and wind instruments such as cornets, flutes, viols and lute (the instrument brought on stage in II.i), as opposed to the trumpets, horns and drums used outdoors. The musicians were probably positioned at the rear of the upper-level balcony, but were able to move forward and be seen when their playing was part of the on-stage action (see IV.i, for example). Certain instruments had particular connotations (flutes or recorders with death, for example), and although there is no hard evidence to support this view, I think 'mood' music would have frequently been used to underscore the language and action, not unlike the way a film score operates today (White 1998: 151–5): Thomas Wilson wrote in 1604 that 'just as certain foods delight the palate, so in music diverse consorts stir up in the heart diverse sorts of joys, sadness and pain'. So it seems likely to me that music was played to accompany scenes, especially those of intense emotional power, and in reading 'Tis Pity we need to be alert to this music-drenched, smoke-filled, candlelit, intimate atmosphere and its impact on our responses to the actions played out on stage.

The 1633 Quarto divides *'Tis Pity* into five acts, which modern editions sub-divide into 27 scenes. At the outdoor playhouses performances were continuous from start to finish, but indoors the act-breaks were required to allow time to trim or replace candles as necessary. They also provided opportunities for the audience to discuss the play with each other, and it is important to remember the effect of these pauses on the rhythm of the play in performance. The majority of the scenes (20) are clearly designated in the text as interior, six as specifically exterior. The interior scenes may be further sub-divided into specific locations: the Friar's cell (2), Florio's house (10), and Soranzo's house (7): this is in all senses a domestic drama. Exterior scenes are precisely placed, too: I.ii, for example, is set on the street immediately outside Florio's house ('What mean these sudden broils so near my doors'), at which point the central stage doors become specifically *his* doors and the upper level represents the window or balcony of his home from which Annabella and Putana observe the scene. III.ix is obviously the street immediately outside the Cardinal's palace and so the central entrance becomes his gates, and (if it was used in the scene) the balcony a position of superiority from which he and Grimaldi can address the citizens. Only III.i is left uncertain, but since scenes are located with such care in the play, I think it evident that it, like I.ii, is set in the street outside Florio's home which Bergetto and Poggio have just left. In all plays performed at the Phoenix the location of the upper level changes during the course of the play (here, in I.ii, III.ii, possibly III.viii and/or III.ix, IV.i) and the same is true of the entrance doors. Act III provides examples of almost all aspects of indoor staging and the text allows us to reconstruct the original performance with some precision. It is an act which uses all the physical resources of the stage and in which candlelight plays a key role in creating and enhancing mood and atmosphere, no doubt underscored by music. As candles took time to extinguish and light their use is often in scenes grouped together. Indications of impending darkness are first given at the close of II.vi when Florio tells us that ''tis supper time, / And it grows late' (123–4), leaving Giovanni and Annabella alone, he looking forward to the pleasures to come: 'Welcome, sweet night! The evening crowns the day' (131). No specific reference to time is given in III.i, but we might imagine that III.ii takes place after supper. The following two scenes, III.iii and III.iv, both also take place in Florio's house, as we move a little further into the night. The action of III.v appears to shift to Richardetto's lodgings (though it may be still set in Florio's house; see p. 50) and more signals are given of the onset of darkness: 'this very night' (8), 'this night' (13), 'a night', (14), 'tonight' (29). All these interior scenes may have seen candles lit to indicate the day closing and night slowly falling. Use of descriptive language such as this is a common practice in the day-lit outdoor playhouses, but indoor performances had the resources to create specific stage states rather than needing to evoke them in the imagination, as the detailed stage direction for III.iv suggests. The stage image created is clearly intended to represent an altar table with the specific reference to 'wax lights', which especially if they are white wax, are the most expensive of all candles, totally different from the general lighting, and therefore designed to make a point. It is possible, too, perhaps, that at this point shutters such as the playwright Thomas Dekker described as being 'clapped up' in a playhouse could be closed, and any readily accessible candles extinguished, to further darken the auditorium. III.vii requires the action to be played if possible in near total darkness, and at this point I believe the chandeliers above the stage, bearing the majority of the illumination, were raised to reduce the level of light on the stage, and the effect would be increased by the wax-lights from III.vi being extinguished at the same time. It is likely too, that as the lighting change is made, suitably atmospheric music was played.

At the start of III.vii, Grimaldi enters carrying a 'dark lantern', which had a device for obscuring its light without extinguishing it. Immediately Grimaldi closes his lantern at the end of his opening lines the stage will again seem even darker than it actually is, since adding a light on stage and then removing it has the effect of making the previous state seem dimmer, even though it has not in fact changed at all. Bergetto and Philotis enter from one of the side doors with Richardetto and Poggio some distance behind. The actual darkness means that it is clear why none of the other characters sees Grimaldi actually stab Bergetto, including Bergetto himself, which adds to his confusion (see pp. 53–4) and the fact that he has to feel his clothes to try to understand what has happened. It is apparent from the text that Richardetto dispatches Poggio for help and lights (back through the door from which they entered, and the opposite of the one Grimaldi fled through) before he moves to Bergetto. It is equally clear that Richardetto's doubt over the extent of Bergetto's injuries results partly from the fact that Bergetto is a bit of a clown, and because neither he nor the audience can see very well. In fact, it is not until Poggio returns accompanied by Officers with lights, and a lantern is either passed to Richardetto or held near him, that the truth of the situation dawns on them. Following the exit of the Officers (the departure of their lanterns again darkening the stage) the mood switches once more for the last moments of the scene. The lighting has been a major agent in creating a sense of confusion as the characters *and* the audience try to work out what's going on, while the hand-held lanterns illuminate the stage action in a more focused way and produce an effect not dissimilar to the *chiaroscuro* (strongly contrasted light and shadow) seen in Caravaggio's or Rembrandt's work, and matching the distinct tones and moods of the action. Now suddenly an expression or gesture (such as Richardetto looking at the blood on his hands) can be caught, as it were, in startling close-up.

# 2 *Commentary: the Play in Performance*

In rehearsal, however well some of those involved might know the text (and everyone will, of course, have read the whole text), it is also important not to get ahead of ourselves but to play (at least at first) only what is happening at that precise moment. What has gone before may, of course, shape the action – but not what is to come. Of course, once we get to the end of the play, we can look back at those earlier signals that prefigured what was to come – some of which we might not have noticed at the time – and, where necessary, adjust. But it is important, I think, to allow unexpected turns in the plot or a character's behaviour to take the performers by surprise, as it were, and see what follows; trying to smooth out what may seem like inconsistencies can often reduce the intentionally complex fabric of a play. So in this Commentary, as far as possible, I have tried not to get ahead of the action, but to wait for events to occur before discussing them. However, as in rehearsal, it is sometimes useful to observe a developing pattern in the action or language of the play, or to pause to consider some wider implication of an idea that the play has raised, or to explore something that helps explain what's going on, or why. I hope the distinction is clear – and that I can keep it that way – as we proceed, so these comments are printed in italics.

In the following analysis, each scene will be divided into smaller units. This is often done in rehearsal to be sure that each section is fully worked through and to help the actors keep focused on the matters in hand. Moreover, as each unit may require a distinctive pace and tone, analysing them separately enables the director and actors to avoid blurring their edges. It is a particularly useful approach with Jacobean plays in general where the shifts of timbre and mood within scenes are often rapid and marked, and where it is vital to avoid erasing these sharp shifts, however awkward or difficult to play they might at first appear. Of course, the thing about plays is that there is no opportunity for the audience, unlike someone watching something on DVD, to rewind to catch something we missed or to fast-forward through the boring bits, or like a reader, to pause to ponder the meaning of a line with the help of a footnote. But in Ford's playhouse the audience did have the chance between each act to chat about the play while the candles were trimmed, so I have also taken that opportunity to add, in some act breaks, and again in italics, a brief reflection on what's happened, how we have moved on, how our understanding and expectations as a reader or audience may have changed.

So, first, the setting of the play: Parma. While only some among Ford's audience may have known that Parma 'was under the domination of the Habsburgs, who had institutionalized incestuous marriages between uncles and nieces as a means of consolidating and maintaining land and power within the family' (Hopkins, 2005: 172), or have heard of, let alone visited the ground-breaking Teatro Farnese built there in 1618, for every spectator the Italian setting would have triggered a whole host of associations. Peter Heylyn articulated these popular prejudices in 1621 when he wrote of the Italians that 'in their lusts they are un-natural, in their malice unappeasable, in their actions deceitful, to which may be added they will blaspheme rather than swear, and murder a man rather than slander him' (quoted in Bowers 1940: 48). Many of those watching would also have been keen to see an allusion to the overarching corruption of the Catholic Church, another prejudice frequently exploited in Elizabethan and Jacobean drama, which acquired particular force in the years around which Ford was writing his play. To many Protestant English men and women the court of Charles I and his Catholic queen, Henrietta Maria, was too sympathetic towards Rome, allowing playwrights to draw a simplistic but nevertheless powerful link between Catholicism and the view of a decadent and corrupt ruling class. Margot Heinemann's (1980) description of Middleton's *Women Beware Women* as a 'city tragedy' is equally applicable to *'Tis Pity*, and Parma is to all intents and purposes London, populated by characters that would be more at home in a Jacobean city comedy than in a conventional revenge play. Indeed, the city itself plays a performative role, contributing to, and in turn being created by, the violence and corruption of its inhabitants, a city so morally deficient that 'individuals find themselves contaminated by a surrounding culture whose spiritual depravity prevents the individual from achieving spiritual transcendence on his or her own' (Amtower, 1998: 84).


# Act I

## Act I, scene i

**0** *Enter* **FRIAR** *and* **GIOVANNI**    The play opens in mid-debate. In Ford's playhouse, with no curtain to raise, once the candles are lit and hoisted up it is left entirely to the actor to harness the audience's attention. It is noticeable how frequently, especially in indoor plays, the opening lines establish the dynamic of the relationships between characters and the circumstances in which the characters find themselves rather than establishing the setting through the words.

**1–12**    The Friar's first line suggests the action is brought on to the stage in mid-flow – this argument has been going on for some time, presumably originating in the confessional – and immediately grabs our interest in exactly what the disagreement is about. The difference in their ages is clear from the Friar's first line (even if the audience doesn't register that 'Giovanni' – pronounced with four syllables – literally means 'young man'), while the Friar's costume will readily identify his role as spiritual adviser. (The Friar's name, we later learn, is Bonaventura, after St Bonaventure, 1221–74, head of the Franciscan order. This suggests that the character probably wears the grey habit of the Franciscan monks, the most common order represented in early modern plays.) The Friar's opening argument establishes the status quo – that beliefs and values must be followed, not challenged. Indeed, this is a dispute in which the questions of one participant are met by the commands of the other, as the Friar dismisses Giovanni's arguments on two grounds: that while it might be possible to advance Giovanni's argument in the context of a hypothetical debate – though we don't yet know what the issue is – to put it forward seriously in terms of specific behaviour would be to defy heaven itself and the order which governs all things. Indeed, he warns (with an echo of the fate of Dr Faustus, echoes that reverberate throughout the play; Hoy

1960) that those overly clever 'wits' who contest the existence of God only discover the reality of hell.

**12–18**  There are no fixed rules that govern how an actor should deliver blank verse, nor do we have a firm idea how the original actors would have done so. But while, understandably, we often focus attention on the words of the plays, especially those that can seem like a foreign language to our ears, the *sound* and the *form* of the language provide vital clues for the actor, such as the use of rhyme, shifts between verse and prose, and, as here, by how lines are allocated between characters. Line 12, for example, is shared between the two characters. This ensures the debate is free-flowing, as Giovanni (his 'gentle' indicating if not agreement, a closeness, even mutual affection between them) insists that he has opened himself up completely by expressing his 'thoughts and heart', and that the Friar has not really responded equally openly to this self-revelation. (See the discussion in the act break before Act II of the significance of 'heart' and other key words in the play.) Indeed, these words with their echo of the penitent at confession (see Woods, 2010) suggest that while Giovanni is prepared to accept the ruling of his priest, he cannot deny the strength of his ideas and his feelings: 'Unbridled emotion and irreverent thought make a dangerous combination' (Stavig 1986: 224).

**19–34**  Giovanni's direct question to the Friar now alerts us to the precise nature of this dispute: why should he not be free to love the woman of his choice? The active 'do' is, as we shall see, a verb Giovanni repeatedly employs, and seems to point ahead to action rather than just an ongoing philosophical speculation on his situation. The answer to the general point is easy for the Friar, but why he should respond so vehemently ('Foolish madman!') to what sounds no more than the kind of excessive claim any young man might make about the beauty of the woman he loves is more puzzling. But the Friar, of course, and we, have no idea what the 'customary form' (i.e., 'normal, common behaviour') in which Giovanni claims the right to share actually is until the bombshell: the object of Giovanni's desire is his sister. Immediately, Giovanni follows up with arguments to support his apparently untenable position: that he and his sister, precisely because they *are* siblings, are bound to be together by the laws of nature, family, reason and, indeed, religion. Of course, this reasoning will be read by most in the audience as an argument proving exactly the opposite, why this desired relationship is unacceptable, and this brilliantly dramatizes the contradiction between Giovanni's and our responses, a tension that Ford pursues throughout the play, between *what* is said and *how* it is said. For example, read aloud lines 30–4, and you can hear how the repetitions driving through the lines mean that while we may reject Giovanni's intellectual arguments, it is much harder for us to deny the sheer force of feeling he expresses.

**35–46**   The Friar sees no way out for Giovanni; if he continues he (and his soul) will be lost. Giovanni seems a mix of certainty and a need for help, first rejecting the idea that he should not pursue his desire (which he makes clear is for a sexual relationship with his sister) and then, sensing a similar conflict in the Friar (in his case between condemnation and compassion), seeking advice on how he might restrain his infatuation.

**47–63**   We now discover more about Giovanni and his relationship with the Friar that helps explain the ebb and flow of the exchanges. We learn that Giovanni was a star student at the University of Bologna (the first to be founded in Europe and where the 'dispute' would have formed a central part of a student's intellectual training), admired throughout the university for his personal and intellectual qualities. Indeed, the Friar himself was so impressed that he gave up his job as tutor to follow his pupil back to Parma. And now, just three months since they arrived, Giovanni has changed out of all recognition. The Friar's warning is ominous: 'death waits on thy lust' (59). His solution, however, is morally compromised at worst, pragmatic at best – Giovanni should seek another lover from all the other beautiful women in the world, which (as a man committed to celibacy) the Friar sees as a loser's game, but nevertheless accepts that pre-marital promiscuity is still less sinful than incest, a venal sin better than a mortal one.

**64–8**   But Giovanni is not to be dissuaded: his passion as unalterable as the powers of nature. His tone of finality clearly impacts on the Friar, who believes him to be doomed. Yet he cannot give up the fight, and the shared line (68) suggests that there is in Giovanni, too, for all his avowed resolution, still a desire to find a way out of this perilous situation.

**69–end of scene**    The Friar sets Giovanni tasks to try to overcome his incestuous cravings: to lock himself away and pray, to be penitent, to confess that his desires make him no better than an animal driven only to satisfy his sexual urges. (This advice is exactly what Robert Burton recommends in his *Anatomy of Melancholy*: 'we must first begin with prayer, and then use physic; not one without the other, but both together'; see Chapter 3, pp. 102–3.) If after a week of this, while the Friar too prays for him, he finds he has not overcome his desire, they will need to think again how he might be cured. Giovanni's final lines are in the form of a couplet, not just a way of concluding the scene, but to underline his commitment. However, they contain doubt: if he cannot free himself from this compulsive love for his sister, and avoid God's vengeance, then he will know that it is his Fate to pursue her, leaving the situation unresolved.

*Thomas Cartelli's view of the early modern audience as a 'receptive auditory', with the ability to respond to the wide 'variety of provocations' offered it from the stage and 'capable of entertaining irreverent attitudes, skeptical opinions, and the most worldly of material ambitions and aspirations' (1991: 64, 61) closely reflects the kind of audience implied by the opening scene and the performance strategies the play will demand as it unfolds.*

## Act I, scene ii

**0 *Enter* GRIMALDI *and* VASQUES, *ready to fight***    The name 'Grimaldi' may draw associations from the Italian word *grimaldelli*, a kind of darting weapon, and an actor might find some value in knowing that; Vasques's name indicates that he is the only Spaniard in the play. The opening of the scene is a mirror of the start of the previous one: two characters come on stage, again presumably both from the same entrance, and as in scene one the opening words ('Come, sir, stand…') suggests that this is not the first line of the exchange. The energetic verbal sparring of the opening scene, carried on formal yet flexible blank verse, and the comparative physical still-ness of the implied staging which focused the spectator's attention on the Friar and Giovanni's opposing arguments, are matched now by rapid, colloquial prose and physical energy and movement. The

costumes of these two new characters will need to distinguish them
as being from different social classes, the distinctions between which
are crucial in the play. (We learn later in the scene, from Bergetto,
that Grimaldi has been a guest at a dinner, explaining the subsequent
references to food: in the 1991 Royal Shakespeare Company (RSC)
production discussed on p. 16 he carried a table-napkin.) The stage
direction indicates they are 'ready to fight', though the subsequent
dialogue suggests that only one of them, if indeed either, has yet
drawn a weapon, since the other is very keen to avoid a skirmish.
The stage direction may, therefore, refer to their physical *and* vocal
manner.

**1–17**  In staging Jacobean plays today, an understanding of the
codes of that society's behaviour can very often be as important
as the more obvious need to understand the language of the plays,
and this section of the scene is an example of that. Superficially, the
exchanges between Vasques and Grimaldi (though we don't learn
the characters' names until Florio and Donado enter at line 20) can
appear to be simply generalized abuse building up to a fight. In fact,
their lines comprise a very precise sequence of insults and would be
read as such by a Jacobean audience, especially one with the social
composition of the Phoenix playhouse (see p. 5). In order to provoke
Grimaldi, Vasques first accuses him of being a coward if he will not
fight, an insult and challenge Grimaldi attempts to deflect on the
grounds that he and his opponent are mismatched both socially and
in terms of skill. Vasques retorts by calling him a braggart. Grimaldi
now develops his original response by identifying in more detail the
social difference between them, claiming that his reputation as a
gentleman would be damaged if he were to fight with an inferior, a
'cast suit' – one whose clothes are passed on to him by his employer.
Vasques responds by upping the level of his insults, calling Grimaldi
a cot-quean (a whore), accusing him of 'scolding' and 'prating' (words
often applied to women; Annabella rebukes Putana for 'prating'
later in the scene), and claiming Grimaldi is in fact inferior even to
Vasques's master's servants. Grimaldi attempts once again to assert
his social superiority: not only is he 'a Gentleman', but one from
Rome – so, by implication, not from some out-of-the-way provincial
town like Parma – and, he repeats, one who has won his 'honour' in
battle.

**18–21**      Vasques's rejoinder is the turning point in the exchange, but we need to fill in some specific contextual material to understand its full force. King James I had issued an edict against duelling in 1614, but the code of honour for a Jacobean gentleman was of greater force. In such situations, as Richard Braithwaite explained in *The English Gentleman*:

> Can any Gentleman suffer with patience his Reputation to be brought in question? Can he endure to be challenged in a public place, and by that means incur the opinion of a Coward? Can he put up disgrace without observance, or observing it, not revenge it, when his very Honour (the vital blood of a Gentleman) is impeached? (1630, quoted in White 1998: 164)

However, finding himself faced with someone who *can*, evidently, endure such a challenge, and clearly frustrated by Grimaldi's stalling, Vasques uses the insult that no gentleman could ignore without losing face: he calls Grimaldi a liar. The fact that playwrights could be certain that their audiences would recognize the significance of this moment is clear from the number of plays – for both indoor and outdoor theatres – that refer to the codes of insult and duel. For example, Shakespeare was sufficiently certain that enough people in the audience at the Globe would understand the code to make it the basis of a comic exchange between Jacques and Touchstone, the clown, in *As You Like It* (V.iv.67–83).

Once this pattern of insult is understood, we will be able to read and perform the section as not merely a bluster of invective, but a conscious and deadly strategy on Vasques's part in keeping with the rules of combat, and with that knowledge the section can be paced accurately. The placing of a pause before the deliberate delivery of the line 'You are a lying coward and a fool', and the way Grimaldi's reception of the insult is played, will ensure that we register its significance. A further bonus may be that the audience laughter that most certainly erupted in the Jacobean playhouse on Grimaldi's desperate line 'Provoke me not' may also be raised in ours.

**22 *They fight*.**      Stage fighting was a popular element of performances, though (unsurprisingly given the more limited stage-space available) less frequent indoors than out. Care was no doubt given to the staging of a fight, not only because of the proximity of members of the audience (especially when they were also seated on the stage), but because further information regarding a character's personality can clearly be revealed through the manner in which he fights (Grimaldi's back-stabbing attack on Bergetto in III.vii is an extension of this).

**23–31**  The rapid pace of the scene continues through the fight until Florio and Donado (with Soranzo) burst on to the stage, their opening lines indicating that they physically pull the two fighters apart, Florio going to Grimaldi, Donado to Vasques. Their lines are basically a series of rhetorical questions couched in fast-moving regular iambics designed to be spoken quickly and vehemently – the repeated 'ee' sound on the stressed words in 'As not to eat or sleep in peace at home', for example, driving the line and the character's energy.

**32–45**  Soranzo's convoluted speech, however, is in marked contrast. Full of parenthetic remarks and multiple clause sentences, it *cannot* be spoken quickly (try it), and it pulls the vocal and physical dynamic of the scene up short. The measured pace of his lines (with perhaps a slightly later entry point than that indicated in the quarto, or a stage position away from the action so far) allows the stage focus to move entirely to Soranzo and changes the pace of the scene completely. These shifts establish Soranzo's control of the stage, and the social hierarchy of the play's world begins to emerge more clearly. No one interrupts Soranzo: he saunters, he addresses whoever he wants, however he wants. It is a speech that swaggers.

On l. 31 Annabella enters (on the upper level at the Phoenix, and often, too, in modern performances) accompanied by Putana, another new character. Annabella's presence performs a number of functions: at last we see the woman who is, we know now, sought after by three men (Giovanni, Grimaldi and Soranzo), and who is the focus of the verbal and physical disputes we have witnessed in the opening two scenes. Soranzo, meanwhile, can use the fact that she witnesses Grimaldi's humiliation to demonstrate further his own moral and social superiority, pointing out again that the Roman's refusal to fight exposes a shameful 'lowness' in his mind. Furthermore, the actors' position on the upper level (or however the staging is achieved in the modern theatre) frames the female character as an object of the gaze of the onstage and actual audience. It is a perspective emphasized by Soranzo's implied gesture (on l. 35) towards 'Signor Florio's daughter', significantly defining Annabella in terms of her relationship to her father rather than by her name (as she will be defined in different roles by the other men who claim control over her). There is, in fact, a double perspective at work here: the audience observe Annabella from their position as audience ('so this is the woman over whom everyone in the play so far seems to be quarrelling!') but, in the following unit (if there has been the interaction with the stage I believe Ford intended), the spectators are also made aware of themselves by Annabella's companion, Putana, as participants in the preceding action. It is another example of how the audience is shifted between engagement and detachment, a particularly potent aspect of this play.

**46–64** The elegance of Soranzo's verbal threat is backed up by Vasques's physical threat to Grimaldi, continuing to take the insulting tone he adopted at the opening of the scene. The 'Spanish blade' is presumably Vasques's own sword, while Grimaldi's 'Remember this' is a threat to Soranzo that the matter is not over. Florio's description of Soranzo's response as a 'storm' may suggest he has by this point lost his temper, as Soranzo makes no effort to reprove Vasques for the way he speaks to Florio (who Soranzo has reason to keep on side) when Florio attempts to calm the mood. Florio, however, can deal with this servant's rudeness unaided. All this heat alerts the audience to an inevitable consequence at some point in the play that the promise of revenge will be fulfilled.

**63–6** Putana is rather like the only member of the audience with a programme, or one who has seen the play before, as she fills in the details on characters and events for everyone in the playhouse. It should be noted that Putana speaks in prose, Annabella in verse, not just because of their different status (though that is a factor), but because of their very different viewpoints on the events and characters they have been watching. (The often-stated view that the distinction between those who speak prose and those who speak verse is a sign of class difference is too generalized and easily challenged; the shift is often a clue that there has been a gear change of some kind in the action.) It is important also to note that in Ford's playhouse,

Putana and Annabella were placed close to members of the audience, visually virtually indistinguishable from those seated either side of them on the upper level.

**67–98**   Putana is Annabella's 'tut'ress' and clearly an echo of Juliet's Nurse, but her relationship with her charge parallels more closely the Friar's rapport with Giovanni. Florio's *World of Words* defined the Italian word 'puttana' as 'a whore, a harlot, a strumpet' and, as she comments on each suitor's physical attractiveness and sexual prowess, her relaxed morality contrasts with the Friar's fire and brimstone warnings of the consequences of immoral behaviour. It is also an opportunity for Ford to fill in some more details about these men we're observing and hearing about. Grimaldi is well built, the nephew of an aristocrat who (counter to Vasques's insults) acquitted himself well-enough in a recent war, though Putana fears that if he were wounded he might now be impaired sexually. Soranzo, on the other hand, is 23 years old and (unusually for an attractive man of his age – though how Putana knows this is not clear) free from venereal disease, as well as being clever, wealthy, generous and nobleman in his own right. Most important, he is sexually accomplished, proved by his adulterous affair with an older woman, Hippolita (now widowed) in her husband's lifetime (widows were often derided for their insatiable sexual desires). Although even the easy-going Putana thinks this liaison might affect his suitability as a possible husband, her 'sardonic voucher for his sexual virility' (in Huebert's sharp phrase; 1977: 83) certainly improves his desirability as a bed-mate from her point of view.

**99–125**   Annabella seems distracted throughout this section and increasingly irritated by Putana's prattling on like someone who's had a drink too early in the day. Undeterred, Putana directs Annabella's (and the audience's) attention back to the main stage on the entrance of Bergetto and Poggio. (This observation scene parallels I.ii in Shakespeare's *Troilus and Cressida* where Cressida watches the Trojan warriors return while her dissolute uncle, Pandarus, comments on their qualities.) Having already compared Grimaldi unfavourably with Soranzo, she now takes the opportunity to dismiss Bergetto as a nonentity (cipher), no more than a fool in fine clothing. Her commentary, mixed with the onstage dialogue, ensures that the audience concentrates in turn on each of the protagonists, and that the foundations of the narrative are well laid. As they watch, taking our focus back to the main stage, the dialogue reveals that Bergetto, Grimaldi and Soranzo have been guests at Florio's where a quarrel has erupted over dinner between the rivals leading to the clash between Grimaldi and Vasques (information that may inform how the opening of the scene is staged). As Bergetto and Poggio exit, the focus moves back to Annabella who reveals that Bergetto too is a suitor. His uncle Donado – Putana suggests – believes Bergetto will be successful because of his prospects as Donado's heir, though she cannot believe that there will ever be such a dearth of penises (bauble = a fool's stick and a penis) to make that prospect necessary.

*At this point, we have encountered the three alternatives to Giovanni that the play offers Annabella – brawling coward, adulterer and idiot. As a result, the attractiveness of Giovanni is made more credible. A small point, but one the actor playing Bergetto – though probably not the audience – may well pick up on: at line 107 Bergetto implies he is an elder brother, something Ford seems to have forgotten by I.iii.62.*

**126–39**  The entrance of Giovanni offers an interesting issue regarding performance, as Annabella actually describes the physical actions she and the audience witness the actor doing. It is evident that in Ford's theatre certain gestures and sounds signified distinct states of mind, and that to beat the breast, weep and sigh were conventional expressions of grief: as John Bulwer noted, in the theatre (as opposed to oratory) 'the Breast stricken with the Hand is an action of Grief, sorrow, repentance and indignation'. While many Jacobean acting signifiers may not match our own and may, consequently, prove difficult for an actor to utilize convincingly, Jonathan Cullen, who played Giovanni in the 1991 RSC production, repeated these precise actions off-stage before he entered, finding they helped generate the physical and emotional energy he needed for the scene.

*The time-scheme of the play is significant but at times unclear. The Friar in Scene i thinks Giovanni is unrecognizable (though that seems to refer to his reasoning), but if Giovanni has followed the Friar's instructions to the letter, and Scene ii takes place one week after scene one, it might explain why he looks in such a distraught state that his own sister mistakes him. Of course, Giovanni's passion may have got the better of his good intentions well before the seven days were up. The difficulty Annabella has in recognizing her own brother is dealt*

*with in Griffi's film (see p. 122) by making it clear that she hasn't seen him since
he returned from university.*

It should be noted that in response to Annabella's remarks, Putana
(who generally only speaks in prose) also speaks verse. Such shifts
are usually for a dramatic purpose, here effecting a change in the
energy on stage as we move from the mundane, social (prose) world
we have just observed, to the intensely personal (verse) relationship
of Annabella and Giovanni.

**140–58**   The first soliloquy of the play. In the intimate environment of Ford's playhouse, even the comparatively low level of light
provided by the candles, perhaps enhanced by some daylight (see p.
6), allowed the actor and audience to make direct contact with each
other, creating moments where a strong engagement, physical and
emotional, between the actors on stage may cause us at moments to
suspend our sense of watching a play. The soliloquy performs two
functions: one, purely practical, is to provide time in Ford's playhouse for the two actors on the upper level to descend to the main
stage via the stairs at the rear of the musicians' space; the second,
in his playhouse and ours, allows us to hear from Giovanni himself
about the events since we last saw him, at the end of Scene i, when
he exited vowing he would conquer his sexual desire for his sister.
Crucially, soliloquies (and other forms of direct address, such as the
aside) enable the actor to forge an empathetic relationship with the
audience or to seek to engage them emotionally and imaginatively in
the stage action. As Giovanni feared, praying has failed to overcome
his love for his sister, his fate has been confirmed and he is lost. But
if Giovanni wishes 'that it were not in religion sin / To make our love
a god and worship it!' (146–7) he is in fact doing precisely that 'by
elevating his passion into his fate and his fate into his deity' (Hogan
1977: 306). With clear-eyed certainty he sees that despite his stren-
uous efforts – weeping, praying, fasting – he is 'still the same' (153).
But as well as *what* he says, we should note *how* he says it: the halting
verse at first (140–2) expressing his uncertainty; then the following
lines flowing with the energy of his prayers, with the size of words –
'judgement', 'endeavours', 'incurable' – embodying the obstacles
in his way; his efforts halted again with the monosyllables of 'but
in vain' (143–5); the semi-assonance and sibilants of 'prayers' and
'tears', set against the harder closing words 'dried up', 'starved'. His

resolution, matched by his rejection of the Friar's warnings, may also challenge the spectator to take a critical attitude to him as Giovanni continues to factionalize those listeners between youth and age – 'I find all these but dreams and old men's tales / To fright unsteady youth (151–2, a significant echo, perhaps of Faustus's dismissal of hell as 'trifles and mere old wives' tales') – before asserting, as he predicted at the end of I.i, that it is his fate which is his master, not his lust: in other words, there is nothing he can do to avert it. But that fate *is* lust. And finally, knowing full well the path he is about to embark on, and consigning 'fear and low, faint-hearted shame' to cowards, he screws his courage to the sticking place and resolves to tell Annabella how he feels, even if the price of doing so is his heart. At this point, Giovanni has marshalled together nature, reason and religion in the defence of incest. It is 'quite a feat, intellectually' (Hogan, 1977: 306), but is an argument full of holes and one which cannot survive the actual experience of making love to his sister.

**159–70** Annabella and Putana join Giovanni on the main stage. Annabella's act of sharing his line indicates the energy with which she enters, while Giovanni's completion of that shared line as an aside suggests his difficulty in encountering her face to face while he summons up his nerve. The 'shape' of the text on the page (in this and the following unit, and itself a useful guide in understanding the performance dynamics) indicates a further change in rhythm of the scene, as it moves into dialogue, with a mixture of short, full-length and shared lines.

**171–202** Following Putana's exit, a section of rapid exchanges (too short to be identified as either verse or prose) shifts into obvious verse for Giovanni (reflecting the emotional level of his expression) intercut with short exchanges from an apparently bewildered Annabella. At l. 187 Giovanni launches into a sensual catalogue of his sister's beauty, each element of which has a double-edge: her forehead is more lovely than Juno's (who was the sister of her husband); her eyes blaze like 'Promethean fire', a conventional image for the beauty of a woman's eyes – see *Love's Labours Lost*, IV.iii.300, for example – but which refers at the same time to the punishment Prometheus received which involved his liver being plucked from his body; and her cheeks are the colour of the lily and the rose (suggesting the fluctuations in her responses to her brother's words). Then Giovanni changes gear, and focuses on her lips, sensual enough to tempt a saint, and on her hands, capable of making even an anchorite 'lascivious', the very sound of the word embracing its sinister meaning. (An anchorite is a celibate hermit; perhaps Giovanni is even unconsciously referring to the Friar here, suggesting that even he, in this situation, might be less certain of his powers of resistance.) This description of Annabella is in the tradition of the 'blazon', a conventional motif in contemporary love poetry, in which the lover catalogues his mistress's beauty by separating out the different parts of her body (see Chapter 3, p. 102). It is, therefore, a rhetorical device more appropriate to a lover than a brother, and some critics have used it as an example of Ford's too-sympathetic portrayal of the lovers. Conventions of contemporary love poetry may not be recognized by an audience now, but their use here is entirely appropriate, given that so far as Giovanni is concerned, a lover is precisely what he is, while their subtext is Ford's way of reminding his audience of the distortion of this self-image.

**203–23** At line 203 a weapon is drawn for the second time in the scene. The sexual imagery is clear: in Giuseppe Griffi's 1973 film version of the play, the lovers grasped the knife together before letting it fall; in a production directed by Jerry Turner for the Oregon Shakespeare Festival in 1981, Giovanni held it phallically erect between them as they knelt; and in the Actors' Company production (1974) he kept the dagger on view throughout their exchange of vows and the long kiss that followed. It seems very likely, too, that for some in the audience the action would have echoed (and still may for an audience today) the moment in *The Duchess of Malfi* when Ferdinand (whose incestuous desires that feed his sexual fantasies are, of course, his alone) threatens his sister with a dagger. In Webster's scene (III. ii), while the sexual imagery is as clear as it is in Ford's, Ferdinand's attempt to 'bring her to despair' is a step towards encouraging the Duchess to suicide, and so associates him with the devilish figures of medieval morality plays determined to damn the Mankind figure by convincing him that God will no longer protect him. This reading is not wholly applicable to this moment in *'Tis Pity* (though Giovanni is encouraging his sister to perform an act that will damn her) but the action of this unit *must* be recalled in V.v when Giovanni again produces a dagger, but this time murders his sister by ripping up *her* bosom to reveal *her* heart. This powerful gesture prompts Annabella to recognize a move from apparent 'game' (pretend) to 'earnest' (real life) in her brother's behaviour. She presumably takes the knife (if his line to her, 'Why d'ee not strike', 214, is to make sense) and we need to remember that through the next section of the scene.

**224–38**  Giovanni tries to convince his sister of his sincerity, wishing that some harm should come to him if he were pretending to love her. But almost immediately, and ominously, he betrays himself to the audience, and this speech is important in establishing his character, and his overriding passion for his sister. In his desire to persuade her of the rightness of their love he invokes the Neoplatonic philosophy that their physical similarity is matched by a corresponding affinity in their souls. But when Giovanni emphasizes that 'Wise nature... meant / To make you *mine*', he revealingly defines Annabella as his possession, while his phrase that nature has given 'one beauty to a double soul' (233) is a distortion of Neoplatonic thinking, which held that for lovers, one soul inhabited two bodies. Still Annabella remains silent, and striving ever harder to convince her, and as his wooing becomes overt temptation, Giovanni tells her what we know to be a blatant lie: that the 'holy Church' (in the form of the Friar) has approved their love. We have not yet seen for ourselves how strongly the Friar's views influence Annabella, but we may assume Giovanni knows that he is distorting the truth. Many critics accept the descriptions of Giovanni as a brilliant student, but surely the university at Bologna taught him to reason better than this. So we can be sure he knows what he's doing, and knows that this is a strong card to play. And he is right, for it is this lie that finally prompts Annabella to make known her choice. These conscious shifts in Giovanni's own reasoning (flaws which would have been perhaps more apparent to many in Ford's audience than ours) and the possessive mentality revealed in his language are all part of a complex characterization which will challenge simple critical partisanship.

**239–end of scene**  Significantly, the line on which Annabella reveals her decision is a shared one:

Giovanni:   Must I now live or die?
Annabella:  Live. Thou hast won

Shared lines should be seen as acting guides, indicating here that there should be no pause before Annabella answers his question. In practice, I have found and observed that actors like to take a pause at this moment while they seemingly make up their mind (as Saskia Wickham did in the 1991 RSC production, for example). If the line is played to follow on seamlessly from Giovanni's, however, it will suggest that Annabella has, in fact, already made her mind up as, indeed, she proceeds to explain she has, and it is consistent with (and explains) the shift in energy she earlier made on seeing her brother (l. 131). It also clarifies for the actor playing Annabella that the preceding dialogue is used by the character to realize not that her brother loves her but that he feels the same as she does, demonstrated in action by the fact that it is she who first kneels to begin their 'betrothal' cere-mony. In other words, the language and action in this short section enable the actor playing Annabella to match, as it were, the aims and energies that, so far in the play, Giovanni has been given more lines and time to express. It enables Ford, in the closing moments of the scene, through a pattern of mirrored gestures and lines, to present an image of two figures equally engaged in thought and action. The physical acts of kneeling (which contrasts with the references in the opening scene), of kissing and embracing (plus the possible translation of dagger into cross) are mediated by Ford's persistence in underlining the familial relationships in the spoken dialogue (the repetitions of 'brother' and 'sister' in particular). The result is a compelling tension between the image and its possible interpretations – betrothal and incestuous union – a tension that informs the entire play. However, as I have noted already, Giovanni from the outset appears to consider his sister as his property, not an individual in her own right, and this attitude reveals itself at numerous moments in the play, not least at its climax. Indeed, it is significant that whereas Annabella swears 'on *our* mother's dust', Giovanni's phrase is '*my* mother's dust', as if his sister 'enables him to have the purest and most complete union of all – a spiritual and physical union with himself' (Lomax 1995: xix) and an example of how Giovanni increasingly draws on the language of triumph to describe his emotional state, language that overrides the search for mutual consent with his sister, and which once trans-formed to physical action, drives its tragic finale.

*As in a number of early modern plays, the absent mother is a significant element that we need to consider. A crucial question for any production, surely,* will be to agree how long it is since the children's mother died, since though she is mentioned only twice and never by name, she is clearly very much still in their minds. Mark Houlahan thinks the reference to 'dust"makes clear she is dead long before the play begins' (2010: 145), but in Jonathan Munby's 2011 production of the play at the West Yorkshire Playhouse the siblings, played by two young actors, were still clearly grieving for their mother, the recent event of her death emphasized by black armbands, a prominent photograph, and so on. When Florio tells Richardetto in II.i that Annabella has 'of late been sickly' (56), which has not been evident from the text, or her behaviour up to that point, Munby's production suggested that Florio interprets her sickness as a symptom of her grief. See p. 119.

## Act I, scene iii

**0–22 Enter FLORIO and DONADO**  We know from the previous scene that Florio is a forceful character who speaks his mind and has a clear sense of his own status. We know too, and he reinforces it now, that while he is keen to see his daughter married, and has apparently assured Soranzo of his support, he appears equally determined at this point not to force her to do so against her will. In his desire to see Annabella marry for love, not money, and to choose for herself, Florio would have appeared notably even-handed to a contemporary audience. As Bianca says in Middleton's *Women Beware Women* (not so different in date from this play), 'Oh, the misery of maids where love's enforced', and arranged marriages are the mainspring of the tragic action in numerous plays of the period. Furthermore, while Florio's readiness to accept his son's apparent indifference to anything but his studies may suggest something of a double standard in his attitudes to his children, the fact that he sees his daughter as the one likely to produce an heir (the pun on 'miscarry' reveals the underlying importance of an heir) makes his apparent willingness not to intervene in her choice all the more remarkable. Of course, the whole scene operates through a screen of dramatic irony as we know that while Donado presses his nephew's case as a suitor to Annabella, she is at this very moment making love to her brother.

**23–8**  Left alone for a moment, Donado provides us with an insight into why he is so keen to see his nephew Bergetto married, and why he has promised to provide him with an annual income of 3000 florins (a substantial but not excessive sum) *immediately* (the meaning of 'presently' in l. 16) and make him his sole heir. But Donado has not much hope that this 'perfect' (the meaning of 'such another') dunce will succeed, and with the arrival of Bergetto we soon understand why.

**28–9 *Enter* BERGETTO *and* POGGIO**   In the 1633 quarto the line 'How now, Bergetto, whither away so fast?' is spoken by Poggio. The implied stage action (confirmed at l. 43) seems to be that Bergetto is rushing across the stage (from one rear door to the other in Ford's playhouse) in his haste to get somewhere, while Poggio, seeing Donado, tries to get his master's attention. Wiggins is the only modern editor to keep the line as Poggio's, all others assigning it to Donado, mainly on the grounds that it would be inappropriate for a servant to address his master by name, and indeed Poggio does not do so at any other point in the play. In the 1630s, 'to podge' meant 'to dawdle', which might hint at why Poggio can't keep up with Bergetto (though 'podgy', meaning plump, and which might help explain his slowness, didn't appear until the nineteenth century). This is the kind of detail in comparing texts that can produce significant bonuses in performance.

**30–44**   Early modern playwrights wrote in what can seem to us at times like a foreign language. Any attempt to minimize the diffi-culties this can present is to no one's advantage, since excavating meanings now obscure to us can produce ideas and interpretations that prove valuable in performance. The problems are particularly notable where humour is involved, which can date very quickly. For example, Bergetto's linking of 'news' and 'mint' is not immedi-ately clear. He appears to be claiming that the news is as reliable as the coins produced at the Royal Mint (then located in the Tower of London), but to Ford's audience 'mint' could also mean a place where things were faked or forged (here a barber's shop; barbers were a notorious source of gossip). A modern audience is unlikely to gather this second meaning nor the actor be able to communicate it, but just the knowledge of the texture in the word might influence the playing in some way. The wonders that have caught Bergetto's imagination smack more of London than Parma. The horse with its tail where its head should be was a common fairground fraud: if you were stupid enough to pay to see it, all you got was the animal tethered by its tail to the manger, where its head would normally be.

**45–end of act**   Bergetto, foolish as he may appear, simply wishes to do what other 'gallants' (fashionable young men-about-town) do: go to see plays, dismissed by his disapproving – or embarrassed – uncle as 'puppet plays' and 'hobby-horses', the kind of joke against themselves that I guess audiences in all periods have laughed at. As with 'mint', however, we need to be alert to another meaning of hobby-horses – prostitutes – and that may be why Donado reminds Bergetto promptly of Annabella. Unable to remember his 'rare speech' to Annabella, Bergetto asks Poggio to relate it. Donado has already expressed directly to the audience (l. 25) that his nephew will need to take lessons if he is ever to win the girl, and this detailed account of the conversation must only confirm his worst fears. However, the conversation Bergetto is referring to must presumably have taken place before the play opened, and to some critics Annabella's question (66–7) sounds distinctly out of character (though it might be a bit early to be certain what that character is). Sturgess suggests that this exchange 'could suggest a stage early in Ford's composition of the play when Annabella was intended to use Bergetto as a cover for her exploits just as Isabella uses the Ward in *Women Beware Women*' (1970: 359). The New Mermaid editor suggests 'parmesan' (58) – 'parmasent' in the quarto – may refer to 'an Italian way of drinking' (*Oxford English Dictionary*), but notes that 'parmesan' gets a bigger laugh in the modern theatre. I think Ford meant it to refer to the cheese and that's why it undoubtedly got a big laugh in the original playhouse, too.

The report of these preposterous attempts to woo Annabella is almost too much for an exasperated Donado, though he becomes much more interested on hearing that Annabella enquired whether Bergetto was his uncle's sole heir. But any expectations are dashed on hearing his nephew's reply (the description of Annabella's response – 'she fell into a great smile and went away' – is especially telling), and a new tactic is required – a letter, written by Bergetto but dictated by Donado, accompanied by an expensive present.

*At l. 14 of the first scene of the opening act, the word 'heart' is heard for the first time, and in its physical and psychological terms and symbolic and literal applications is used 43 times in the play (not counting words such as 'sweetheart'). The heart was an especially potent image for Ford and his* contemporaries: the ritual act of an executioner cutting out the victim's heart removed, in effect, both the actual and symbolic centre of the individual, a performative act that demonstrated to the spectators that the state could possess and, if it chose to, obliterate that individual. It was on the heart, too, that the true feelings and experiences of a person were believed to be inscribed. When one of Queen Elizabeth I's ladies in waiting died, apparently from grief at the death of her brother, the Queen ordered her body to be 'opened' to discover the cause of her death, when she was found to 'have certain strings striped all over her heart'. Ford's plays frequently engage with this central metaphor of the heart as the core of true feeling; it pervades The Broken Heart, where as Calantha dances, news is brought to her in turn of 'death, and death, and death', the 'silent griefs which cut the heart strings… Crack, crack!' (V.iii.87). And in Ford's Love's Sacrifice, another play of illicit but heartfelt love, Fernando tells Bianca, that 'If, when I am dead, you rip / This coffin of my heart, there shall you read / With constant eyes, what now my tongue defines, / Bianca's name carved out in bloody lines' (II.iii.98–101). One of the most pervasive emblems of the time was 'Love's Torment', the image of a heart pierced with a weapon, an arrow or dagger. In Spenser's epic poem The Faerie Queen, for example, a sadistic Cupid contrives a bloody masque in which 'a most fair Dame' appears, a deep knife wound in her breast, 'That dyed in sanguine red her skin all snowy clean' and 'At that wide orifice her trembling heart / Was drawn forth, and in silver basin laid, / Quite through transfixed with a deadly dart' (Book III, Canto XII, 19–21). The 'heart' as an active emblem of the interiority or essence of a person will recur throughout the play (I.i.14, 22; I.ii.54, 206, 241; II.i.5, 32; II.ii.36; II.iii.49; III.ii.24, 35; III.vi.32; IV.ii.7; IV.iii.53–4, 108, 119, 127; V.iii.11–12; V.v. 56, 78, 103; V.vi.2, 16, 26–7, 30, 45, 59, 61, 72 – the greatest cluster is in the final scene), and it will be important each time to note how we read it differently as a result of the developing action. Throughout, Ford repeats such key words, allowing them to shift between the different meanings they could have for his audience. The most repeated word in the play is 'know', which in different forms occurs over one hundred times, reminding us how important ideas around knowledge and ignorance are in the play. 'Blood' occurs more than thirty times, and is a particularly potent example, with its meanings of 'sexual passion', 'life force' and 'high birth' (which has significant implications for the class conflicts in the play). Although we might only become gradually aware of these patterns (so that the irony of the premonition in Giovanni's closing lines of his soliloquy that it is his heart that will ultimately be the price of his pursuit of Annabella, may only resonate fully in retrospect) we need to be alert to these vibrating words as we work on the play.

# Act II

## Act II, scene i

o *Enter* GIOVANNI *and* ANNABELLA, *as from their chamber* The stage direction indicates that the characters enter in some way (they might also be dressing, or adjusting their clothes) that indicates to the audience where they have come from, in this case the room (probably bedroom) where they have been making love. But 'chambering' is an Elizabethan word for sexual indulgence, which offers an interesting take on how they might be behaving. (See Dessen 1985: 40–2 for discussion of costume and its significance in the early early modern playhouse.)

1–15 The tone is light, full of laughter. This could be any young couple after their first love-making together (and will have an added resonance for any in the audience who remember the dawn parting of Romeo and Juliet; III.v). But from the opening line Ford ensures that the audience keeps the lovers' actual relationship in mind, so maintaining the tension between language and subject of earlier scenes. Giovanni's opening lines demonstrate how he sees the fundamental relationship between them to have changed, whereas we will note that he has simply shifted the terms of the relationship with his sister, a relationship which cannot, of course, be altered. Giovanni teases his sister, but she is right to remind him that while it may be 'well' for him, female virginity is a priceless commodity in the marriage market. It may not be immediately obvious why she describes his line 'Music as well consists / In th'ear as in the playing' as 'wanton' (13–14), but he is arguing that you don't have to be able to play a musical instrument in order to appreciate the beauty of the music it makes. (I have been unable to trace the source of the note by the Routledge editor Simon Barker that 'ear refers to the female genitalia' (1997: 141), and although in the seventeenth century 'ear' *was* used to refer to one of the auricles of the heart, and the heart is a central emblem in the play, I can't imagine this helps the actor, audience or reader.)

16–20 It is often suggested that as youths played the female roles on the Jacobean stage the physical contact between lovers was played down, but the texts of the plays often challenge this assumption. Here, Giovanni's use of 'hung' and 'sucked' to describe their kiss suggests a very lingering, sensuous moment between them. The lovers' passion is acted out in poetry 'whose very lyricism is ironic' (McLuskie, 1981: 209) as is its subject matter, and we need to be especially alert to the classical reference Ford employs here, as there is a clear sub-text. When Jupiter, the king of the gods – whose wife, Juno, was also his sister – wanted to make love to Leda, he came to her in the shape of a swan, and seduced her. The story was popularized in Elizabethan England by George Golding's English translation of Ovid's *Metamorphoses*, and was a common subject in Renaissance sculpture and painting. The image has continued to fascinate artists and writers since, many of whom have emphasized the erotic and phallic aspects of the image and its reminder that unnatural love is doomed. Giovanni seems caught up in the whole image, too, revealing a triumphant possessiveness 'in being king' of Annabella and indeed, his virtual self-deification in casting himself as a human rival to Jupiter, 'More great than were I king of all the world' (20). His lines (as elsewhere in the play) seem to echo those in a poem by John Donne, here 'The Sun Rising', included in Donne's *Songs and Sonnets*, published the same year as the play: 'She is all states, and all princes, I, / Nothing else is' (21–2).

**21–5**  At this point, when the reality of their situation intrudes, the abruptness of the shift in Giovanni's language embodies the collision between their private love and the public world they must move in. Here, however, with the use of 'have you' (23) the sexual reference is completely clear, both to us and the Jacobeans who also used the phrase in the sense of 'possessing sexually'. Equally shared is the verb's aggressive tone, as Richard III uses it of Lady Anne: 'I'll have her – but I will not keep her long' (I.ii.230). This vocabulary and their shared lines reflect the urgency of the exchange, while her reference to crying 'in earnest' (the term Jacobeans employed to contrast with 'in game', or 'play') may suggest that she has pretended to cry while they bantered with each other only moments before, and the arrival of real tears signals the shift in mood and temperature of the scene.

**25–32** The actor will need to decide whether Giovanni has deliberately been testing Annabella, trying to draw a response from her, or
whether he is telling it as he sees it. Whichever choice is made, her
tone, her evident distress at his words, clearly pulls him up short, and
he seizes on the possibility that her fierce denial reflects her true feelings and intent, their repeated use of 'dare' underlining that they each
recognize the risk they take in making such a commitment to 'live to'
(i.e. be faithful to) each other. (And we might recall this moment in
Giovanni's exchange with Vasques in V.iii.45–54 which hinges on the
repeated use of 'dare'.)

**33–6** Line 33 is made up of five monosyllables and stands out in
the midst of a flow of regular iambic pentameters (i.e. ten syllable
lines). The missing syllables suggest a pause, presumably to reflect
Annabella's surprise that at this particular moment Giovanni is leaving.
Many critics have noted Ford's skilful use of silences, as here, making
the moment particularly arresting, and suggesting Ford is keen to
impress it on us. At the same time, the abruptness of 'I must' indicates
the imperatives to which their love, however strong, is subject.

**37–48 *Enter* PUTANA** It is often suggested that prose is the
medium of comic or 'lower class' characters, or servants. In fact, there
are no rules about who can or cannot employ either verse or prose,
but the shift from one to another *is* invariably a clear indication that
there is a gear-change of some kind. Here, the change is made more
emphatic by the sustained, unbroken verse lines that precede it.
While Annabella appears to continue in verse (though all her lines
except 39–40 are too short to be sure) Putana speaks in prose not
because (or not only because) she is a servant, but because her lines,
however amoral they might appear to be, do in fact spell out the
situation as it actually is. Her explanation that the driving force is no
more than a sexual itch that must be scratched may not at this point
do justice to what we have just seen of the obviously loving relationship between brother and sister (and we may recall the difference
here between her and Juliet's Nurse in a parallel moment (*Romeo and
Juliet*, III.v.218–24), but the repeated references to 'lust' must create a
tension in our response.

**49–51** Florio's voice from offstage is an intrusion of the world from which their secret must be kept if a scandal ('the speech of the people') is to be avoided. The pathetic yet realistic scrabble for Annabella's sewing, in order to present an image of domestic normality to Florio and the guests, brilliantly captures the double-life Annabella now must lead.

**52–end of scene** Two new characters are now introduced: a 'doctor of physic' and a young woman. In Ford's day, there was a hierarchy of the medical profession, with physicians at the top and surgeons, barbers and apothecaries below them; this one evidently comes from Padua, a city 80 miles north-east of Parma renowned for its university's medical school (and, significantly, for its anatomy theatre, see pp. 100–1). On the Jacobean stage the physician would have been recognizable from his costume and, in this case, as we learn later (II. vi.83), he also sports a 'broad' (i.e. large) beard. He is accompanied by his 'kinswoman… a maid', who carries a lute. (You can see and hear lutists perform music contemporary with this play on YouTube.) It is not quite clear how Florio met this doctor and his niece, and though we do not yet know their names, the detailed introduction they receive suggests they will play a significant part in the action. The fact that Florio thinks his daughter has been unwell also comes as news to us (and it's important we don't miss this information), while the doctor's reference to Annabella's reputation for virtue and 'perfection' (in beauty, accomplishments, etc.) may now have an ironical edge to it for the audience. Similarly, what an audience may take as the double meanings in 'touch an instrument' ('play the lute'/'handle a penis') emphasize that Annabella is now open to this kind of wordplay: she now must play a part, and that part has a sub-text.

*This point in the play marks the close of the first 'movement'. The basic conflicts have been presented and established. Now they must work themselves out, and Ford allows the world that surrounds the Annabella and Giovanni to take prominence. Although their relationship is not allowed to move from our thoughts, and although we obviously don't know it yet, we will not see the lovers alone together until V.v, apart from a brief moment at the end of II.vi. Having set the central plot running, and introduced all the potential suitors, Ford at this point moves to establish in more depth the wider social context in which Giovanni and, in particular, Annabella must negotiate their secret relationship.*

## Act II, scene ii

**0** *Enter SORANZO in his study, reading a book*   The direction for a character to 'enter in' some location or other is very common in early modern plays. Modern editors are fond of explaining a stage direction such as this by referring to a 'discovery space' or some such recess at the rear of the stage. However, recent experiments on reconstructed outdoor and indoor stages (see White, 2009) have demonstrated that this is an unlikely solution. More probably, as in this instance, the actor enters a space which moments before was a room in Florio's house and is now the study of someone we recognize – the nobleman Soranzo. He is reading. The 'smooth licentious poet' (4) is the Neapolitan Jacopo Sannazaro (1456–1530), whose portrait by Titian is in the Royal Collection. Sannazaro's *Arcadia* – appropriately in these circumstances a story of frustrated love – would have been well known to many in Ford's audience, and had inspired Sir Philip Sidney's work *The Countess of Pembroke's Arcadia*, one of the most famous poems of the age. The mention at l. 15 of Sannazaro's 'encomium' refers to the poet's six-line epigram in praise of Venice, probably his most famous work in England. At l. 9 it appears Soranzo writes his own version of Sannazaro's poem, which suggests that some items – a writing desk, a few books, perhaps a candle, as specified in stage directions in other plays (Dessen and Thomson 1999) – have been set at the opening of the scene, to indicate a study.

**1–18**   The lines from Sannazaro that Soranzo quotes might be more a motto for Giovanni and Annabella's situation rather than reflecting his own experience. Indeed, unlike Giovanni who expresses his passion as freely as he feels it, Soranzo appears, by comparison, guarded, even superficial: certainly the images on which he draws are conventional, reflected in the measured, organized and regular nature of this speech.

**19–60**   The sound of Vasques's raised voice off-stage interrupts this mood of erotic contemplation, followed by a woman, dressed in black, bursting on to the stage, and completing Soranzo's line as she enters. At l. 44 Soranzo identifies the intruder as Hippolita. It is possible that alert members of the audience will register her as the 'lusty widow' referred to by Putana in I.ii, with whom Soranzo 'purchased such a good name... in her husband's lifetime' (I.ii.95–6). The energy and passion of her lines, the speed of her speech (not easy in terms of punctuation and breathing: try ll. 68–81, for example), the sequence of imperatives ('Look, perjured man', 'Know, Soranzo', 'Call me not dear', etc.) and rhetorical questions, extravagant imagery and the interjection of half-lines by Soranzo over which she drives on all create a sense of the hostility she feels for him as she accuses him of having seduced her (we might imagine he's culled a few good lines from his reading of Sannazaro). We hear now more detail of the relationship between them and the circumstances of her husband's death, as she confesses she had a relationship with this young man while her husband (whose death was 'urged on by his disgrace' (40) at his cuckolding), was alive, and now accuses Soranzo of infidelity by rejecting her. Her sense of having been wronged is driven by her guilt at her own actions but perhaps more fiercely by the fact that he now desires someone else: the social competitiveness that suffuses the play is brilliantly exposed in her sneering, snobbish dismissal of Annabella as 'Madame Merchant' (49). But as with the scenes between Annabella and Giovanni we need to be careful to keep the full picture in our heads, to see the simultaneous layers in the scene.

**61–5**  As the row reaches a crescendo, Vasques intervenes, speaking prose, which marks a change of tone as he tries to calm things down. First he hints to Hippolita that Soranzo might have had plans to recompense her in some way and that her behaviour might now thwart ('unedge') that. Turning to Soranzo, he points out that he should understand that Hippolita's behaviour is driven by grief at her husband's death and that having had a chance to vent her feelings a more rational exchange between them might now be possible.

**66–94**  Soranzo's fierce rejection of what he sees as Vasques's disloyal attempts to intervene sets Hippolita off again. But this time she is more coherent in her attack, calling on Soranzo to deny the oath he made to her that he would marry her if and when she became a widow, a vow which led her to encourage her husband to make the dangerous journey to Livorno, a sea-port on the Mediterranean coast about a hundred miles south-east of Parma, across difficult mountainous, outlaw-infested country. And, she tells us, it was on this journey that (but not how) he died; now we have a clearer idea

what is driving her guilt and ratcheting up her sense of betrayal by
Soranzo. It also confirms that she, like Giovanni and Annabella, is
not the victim of a blind passion, however strong the sexual attraction she felt for Soranzo, but that she also embarked on the affair
deliberately and fully aware of the implications; in both the main and
sub-plots, characters choose their courses of action, though often
invoking Fate as the cause. Soranzo's response, however, is to deny
any responsibility on his part, and to claim that any vows he might
have made were more sinful to keep than break, given that she was
a married woman. Soranzo's shifty reasoning added to his pious
claims to virtue, while behaving anything but virtuously, are particularly obnoxious characteristics. Indeed, he not only maintains that
he is penitent, but rubs salt in the wound by listing the considerable
virtues of the husband she betrayed.

**95–100**   This brazen, provocative statement (we certainly have seen
no evidence of Soranzo's contrition) is too much even for Vasques,
who rebukes his master for stirring things up. But Soranzo has had
enough: now Hippolita is a 'monstrous', 'foul' and sinful woman who
he would rather die than have anything to do with. He exits without
waiting to hear if she has any response to make.

**101**   In early modern plays, comparing a character's behaviour to
an actor's performance is a common way of calling in question its
genuineness. So Vasques's description here of Soranzo's behaviour
as 'scurvily played' suggests not only that his master has failed to
follow his advice, but confirms to us that Soranzo's claim to have
seen the error of his ways is a posture. The theatrical analogy forms
part of a pattern in which characters throughout the play consciously
or unknowingly present themselves in a particular 'role' or observe
their own behaviour.

**102–40**   Hippolita's lines indicate that far from needing Vasques's
reassurances of his opinion of his master, she is clear about her own
course of action: revenge (to add to the threat already made against
Soranzo by Grimaldi in I.ii). As she goes to leave, Vasques calls her
back. He tries to convince her that she was too fierce in her manner,
that Soranzo was in a particularly bad frame of mind and that he
will be in a different mood the next day. As Vasques points out,

her response is unhelpfully sarcastic, but at that point, in an aside (not marked in the original text but implied) she realizes something to her advantage. Her tactic now is to try to turn Vasques against Soranzo, implying that Soranzo can drop him as easily as he has her, and she moves (with startling suddenness given her claims earlier of the chasteness of her bosom) to imply not only financial rewards if Vasques will change allegiance, but sexual favours too. She presses the financial insecurity he faces, repeating her astonishing promise of nothing less than marriage.

**141–3**    Hippolita's rapid volte-face has (unsurprisingly) not fooled Vasques, as he confides in an aside (again implied). His description of her as an 'old mole' directly echoes *Hamlet* (I.v.164) where the prince likens his father's Ghost to an engineer burrowing to undermine a fort's defences. So here, too, Vasques sees Hippolita as scheming to undermine Soranzo, while the fact that the mole cannot see carries the sense of her stumbling blindly in to a trap as Vasques hunts her (the sense of 'having the wind', or scenting her).

**143–end of scene**    Vasques now sets his trap. Believing that he has taken the bait and that she is in the driving seat, Hippolita goes further. She takes his hand, which may imply she wants to shake on their deal. But it might carry a greater meaning, one that would cast the lines that follow as a vow (a version of that between Giovanni and Annabella and perhaps the pledge to her by Soranzo), made in the sight of heaven, as she offers Vasques, a servant – this, remember, is the woman who dismissed Annabella as a suitable match for Soranzo – not just money, but also herself and her estate: in effect a promise, without actually saying the word, of marriage. ('Handfasting', the clasping of hands, was, in effect, a formal confirmation of a couple's betrothal; see III.vi.51–2.) Indeed, it seems so unlikely that Vasques accuses her of being 'merry' (i.e. joking, Annabella used the same word in I.ii), in making a vow which (with no irony) he neither thinks nor believes to be true. Significantly, Vasques describes himself as willing to be a 'special actor' in her plans, a clear signal that he is only performing this new role of revenger and prospective husband. We are therefore unlikely to share the confidence she has in her success at setting in train the death of Soranzo, and, to Ford's audience, her reference to 'banquet' will point to the possible site of the act itself.

*The last section of the scene between Hippolita and Vasques raises the question of the form and function of Asides, though many of those marked in modern editions are not signalled in original manuscripts or printed editions. In The Taming of a Shrew (published anonymously in 1594), we find the direction 'she turns aside and speaks' which may suggest a particular way of delivering the aside. Certainly, as my own experiments in a reconstructed early modern indoor playhouse have shown, these moments are a form of staged subtext, reminding us that while we may become caught up in the emotional drive of the play, it is also possible to keep us, at the same time, alert to the play as play. Furthermore, they act then as miniature soliloquies, revealing a character's inner thoughts and so challenging us to take an attitude to the speaker. If the asides are not played directly to the audience, the actor is faced with having to find a way to include this moment of talking to him or herself within an otherwise 'naturalistic' scene. In the 1980 television version of the play (see pp. 127–32), the asides were omitted, with the effect in this instance of not only making Vasques's subsequent actions as much as a surprise to us as to Hippolita, but also denying the audience the full understanding and enjoyment of the means by which different characters chart their way through the play.*

## Act II, scene iii

**0 *Enter* RICHARDETTO *and* PHILOTIS**   Some modern editions add to Ford's stage direction that Richardetto is still in his physician's garb (the 'borrowed shape' Philotis refers to). However, theatrically, we need to see that it is, indeed, borrowed, which suggests that while the disguise is visible on stage, Richardetto is not fully dressed in it, or perhaps he is just not wearing the beard. Given the regularity with which early modern actors doubled, or even trebled, parts we also need to be clear that this is one character with two roles, rather than one actor with two parts. The word 'shape' carries connotations beyond simply the form of the body, being used specifically to refer both to an assumed appearance and to the character impersonated by an actor, and the costume and make-up suited to that part.

**1–16**   Richardetto's opening lines may puzzle us, as they do his niece, while his answer to her question lets another part of the puzzle drop into place: this is Hippolita's husband, Philotis's 'wanton aunt', though he has no idea that Soranzo's defection has brought an end to their 'lascivious riots' and 'loose adultery'. Philotis supposes his journey to Parma is to wreak 'some strange revenge' (another plot targeting Soranzo), but he declines to tell her more, as not knowing anything of his plans will protect her from future accusations of being implicated in his actions.

**17–27**   Questioned by her uncle about the time she spent with Annabella, Philotis proves to be a shrewd observer and judge of others, having identified Annabella's lack of interest in not only Soranzo but seemingly any other suitor on offer, the cause of which, as Richardetto notes, is a 'mystery' which will be revealed in time. His line 'I am the doctor now' (26) may suggest he has been donning his disguise throughout the scene, or that on hearing someone approach he has put his false beard back on.

**28–38** *Enter* **GRIMALDI**   The stage direction in the original printed text is placed after Richardetto's 'But who comes here?', though some modern editors – finding the idea of Grimaldi standing on stage in full view of the audience while Philotis describes him an unconvincing one – put his entrance later, and imagine a solution such as Philotis peering to see who has knocked. However, the staging implied by the quarto text is not at all impossible; it is a device found elsewhere in early modern plays to have characters describe others already on stage but not fully 'in the scene' (see *The Duchess of Malfi*, I.i.148–200, or *Henry VIII*, III.ii, for example). Richardetto repeats what we learned in I.ii – that Grimaldi is a Roman and a soldier, and 'near allied' to the Duke of Monferrato (in fact he's his nephew), so confirming Grimaldi's claims about his social status. However, he adds a crucial piece of new information: Grimaldi intends to use his links to the Pope's representative in Parma to help him secure Annabella's 'love'.

**39–end of scene**   Left alone, Grimaldi (who though known to Richardetto doesn't recognize him) asks if the doctor can provide some potion to make Annabella fall in love with him. But Richardetto has other plans, telling Grimaldi that potions are pointless while Soranzo lives, given that in the contest between these suitors to possess Annabella's heart, Soranzo has already won (a lie, as he has

just learned from Philotis), and moreover (as Grimaldi may know
already) is also favoured by Florio to be his son-in-law. Line 55 is
puzzling. Some editors link it to l. 54 ('take my advice for the cardinal's sake'), others as leading to the following lines, suggesting that
Richardetto offers to help kill Soranzo as a favour to the Cardinal
(which hardly casts the church in a positive light). Richardetto may
think that he can in this way distance himself from any inference
of a personal motive, but the fact that his plan is for Grimaldi to
kill Soranzo with the poisoned sword (an echo of *Hamlet*) is clearly
premeditated, and his comparison of Soranzo to the Hydra (a mytho-
logical many-headed venomous monster) reveals his personal motive
and his pleasure at the prospect of revenge – just for the audience if
GRIMALDI exits after 'yourself' – in the closing couplet.

## Act II, scene iv

**1–18**   The play's structure of juxtaposing characters and events
and actions continues, a strategy that constantly challenges us to
rethink our attitudes. Soranzo has read Sanazar, now Bergetto reads
(through Poggio) his own love letter rather than the one that has
evidently not only been dictated by Donado, but written out by him
too, as Bergetto argues that Annabella will not believe a letter in
someone else's handwriting.

**19–end of scene**   Bergetto's letter is hopeless; obscure in its
meaning, charmless and littered with (intentional?) *double-entendres*
referring to sexual intercourse: 'lie' (as in *Hamlet*), 'board' (with an
added homonym, 'bourd', meaning to jest), 'my best parts' and
'upwards and downwards'. Donado's exasperation with his nephew
is understandable, but Bergetto's guileless interest in pursuing the
attractions of the fair rather than those of the 'fair' Annabella means
we can see him as harmless, even likeable, in contrast to the aggressive behaviour of the other suitors.

## Act II, scene v

**1–26**   The tone radically changes as the Friar and Giovanni enter.
In rehearsal, playing just the scenes between the Friar and Giovanni
would be a useful exercise to help chart the line of Giovanni's shifting
mental and emotional state and the increasing gap opening between

the two men. The start of the scene, with them both in mid-argument, recalls the beginning of the play, but (as we know from I.ii and II.i) the situation has radically altered. The Friar has fulfilled his part in trying to rescue Giovanni from his fate, but now he sees Giovanni as damned, reminding him (9–11) of his warning in I.i of the divine justice that waits on sinners. For his part, elated by the discovery that Annabella welcomes this 'forbidden' love, Giovanni advances his arguments to prove it is both 'fit and good'. He does so through a series of 'twisted Platonic jargon' (Stavig 1968: 104), building his argument on a series of premises, without proving any, to conclude with a 'proof'. The exposure of such fallacious reasoning would have been part of the course in logic he studied at university, so confirming Giovanni must know exactly what he is doing.

**27–39**    Giovanni's argument is countered by the Friar's dismissal of this false analysis as unfit for modern thinkers, and his disagreement with the notion of a man being led as were the philosophers of earlier times by 'Nature's light' rather than acceding to God's laws, which are not open to dispute or question. Giovanni moves to a more personal argument: that the Friar is too old to understand how he, a young man in love, feels, even blasphemously elevating his and Annabella's passion to a religion. The rhyming couplets that complete the Friar's speech (33–4) and form Giovanni's response (35–6), no longer shared, indicate how absolute each is in his attitude, and prompt the Friar to concede his impotence in trying to persuade Giovanni to repent.

**39–58**    Seeking a way out of this seeming impasse, the Friar now moves to a more pragmatic strategy: that Annabella must marry. This is rejected by Giovanni on the moral grounds that for her to do so would make his sister in effect an adulteress, and we notice how incest is moving in Giovanni's mind to be a state of normality. The Friar then asks that he should be allowed to hear Annabella's confession, but in response Giovanni almost mockingly offers a sensual (if conventional) description of her beauty (blonde hair was considered an exceptional feature at the time) and its impact on him. As in I.ii, he again employs the technique common to love poetry, the 'blazon', in which the lover separates out the parts of the woman's body – here, face, lips, eyes, hair, cheeks – and which, though it appears as a mode of praise, may also be seen as a way for the man to master 'his lady by inscribing her in a text, constructing and dismembering her, part by body part' (Traub 1992: 40). But in contrast to the conventions of Petrarchan love poetry, which specifically avoids reference to the woman's 'other parts' (see p. 102 for a classic example of the genre), the unconcealed sexual imperative in Giovanni's desire for his sister is underlined by the titillating reference to the sexual pleasure her body has given him.

**59–end of scene**     In the opening scene of the play, lines shared between these two characters embodied their mutual search for a solution to Giovanni's situation. Here, a shared line first raises the possibility of an understanding (63) before dashing that hope and emphasizing the gap between them (65). It is crucial that an audience registers the Friar's fears that in Giovanni's desire to supplant his hopes of heaven and salvation with his love for Annabella, to find all completion in her, brother and sister both risk eternal damnation, and the loss of their souls, his certainty underlined by the couplet that concludes the scene (though it will not rhyme in modern pronunciation).

*As an audience we are aware of the contrast between this and the opening scene, and the effect of the intervening action. Now we know of the simple but harmless Bergetto; the pragmatism of Florio and Donado; the self-regarding adulterer Soranzo; the deceptions and intrigues of Hippolita and Richardetto. This awareness creates a fuller perspective from which we observe Giovanni and Annabella. This is not to say that in contrast to the world that surrounds them their love – in its way pure and committed – appears justified. In fact, in developing the action, and in his very precise use of language and literary strategies such as the blazon, Ford neither excuses nor condemns the lovers, but by seeing them in a wider context and how others respond to them, he allows us to 'accommodate' their love for each other while still maintaining a critical attitude to them, the strength of which will derive from our individual responses and moral standpoints.*

## Act II, scene vi

**1–59**     Whatever Giovanni or Annabella's thoughts on marriage, the market is still busy. With Bergetto absent at the fairground, a letter is presented to Annabella. It is not clear whether it is the one read in II.iv, as despite her father's request to read the letter aloud,

Annabella reads it only to herself. But she makes no reference to the bizarre contents of Bergetto's letter so it seems more likely it is Donado's version. Putana (who we remember has already been paid by Soranzo to further his cause) is remunerated now by Donado for (so she says) promoting Bergetto's candidacy, while Florio too can appear to press Bergetto's cause enthusiastically, presumably confident that his daughter will resist the offer. Nevertheless, it may seem he takes the effort unnecessarily seriously (and feels a bit like a rather clumsy bit of plotting on Ford's part) when he suggests that she should send Bergetto a ring bequeathed her in her mother's will, with an injunction that she should only part with to her husband. This is the ring she earlier gave Giovanni (perhaps we should actually see this performed in I.ii), and Ford's audience would undoubtedly see the ring's significance, common in Ford's plays (see especially *The Broken Heart*, IV.i.23–34), plus its possible sexual reference to the vagina (the same meaning underlies exchanges at the opening of *The Duchess of Malfi*). That particular resonance is not picked up, of course, by her father, but dramatically the moment is a particularly awkward one for Annabella. Florio, however, appears to accept without question her reason for not having it with her (perhaps supporting an interpretation of their mother's recent death), and proceeds to ask whether or not she is interested in Bergetto. Her 'plain dealing' answer impresses Donado who, it appears, acknowledges that this is the end of these particular negotiations.

**60–115**  Bergetto has been injured while avoiding a possible duel (he is as alert to the niceties of the challenge as Vasques and Grimaldi; see I.ii and Commentary). His assailant tried to provoke him by forcing him away from the wall – the driest place to walk, away from the drain in the middle of the street that carried all waste – and pushing him, too. The upshot is clearly what Vasques hoped his insults to Grimaldi in I.ii would achieve, and Grimaldi was lucky that Richardetto heard the fray and took him into his house and bandaged him up. Perhaps Grimaldi removes his hat to reveal it on 'look you, here 'tis', or possibly it has been visible all the time (though no one has mentioned it) and the joke is that Bergetto indicates something blatantly obvious to everyone. More important for Bergetto, however, he met Philotis, who has taken his fancy, and – despite the fact he has come woo Annabella – he now declares he will 'love her as long as I live'. You can almost hear Donado's despairing sighs as Bergetto continues, amiably, to dig himself a deeper hole, affirming that Philotis is 20 times more beautiful than Annabella.

**116–23**  As Bergetto, Poggio and Donado depart, Giovanni enters. Florio, agreeing with his son that Bergetto was never a serious candidate for Annabella's hand, confirms once more his preference for Soranzo.

**124–end of act**  Left alone, mention of Soranzo appears to trigger Giovanni's jealousy, despite his sister's incredulity at his response and joking tone. The lines are shared between the two, allowing the energy of Giovanni's questioning and Annabella's rebuttals to move appropriately fast. But the last two lines of the scene remind us that for all the business with letters and banter over jewels, this relationship between brother and sister is an intense and passionately sexual one. This short section at the end of the scene is important. It is the first time since the beginning of the act that we have seen the lovers alone. She teases. He is jealous. They are moving at different speeds in different worlds.

# Act III

## Act III, scene i

**1–end of scene**  With only 23 lines, this is the shortest scene of the play. Bergetto, having found and fallen for Philotis, is determined to take his own decisions rather than be led by his uncle. In a sense, Bergetto finds himself in a situation similar (though very different in scale) to Giovanni; a relationship about which, as Poggio, observes, secrecy must be maintained (though Donado did not appear particularly opposed in II.vi, telling Bergetto he was now 'free'). For the performers, however, a more immediate issue will be how to make sense of the often impenetrable lines that are clearly intended to be funny but in which the joke is hard to locate, even more difficult to deliver. For example, no modern edition offers a gloss on 'in despite of his nose' (5), and I cannot offer one either. On the other hand, the various explanations offered for Bergetto's last lines (21–3),

while helpful to the reader, may not help the actor; you can't act a
footnote.

## Act III, scene ii

**1–10**   With Bergetto out of the running, and Grimaldi seemingly no
longer under consideration, Florio has just one remaining suitor for
his daughter, and that's his own preferred choice. But he still sounds
like the merchant he is, making sure that Soranzo recognizes that
there have been plenty of other offers. The word 'jointure' is interesting here, carrying the senses of a union, but also of a legal binding
of two estates: in this case the merchant's money with the aristocrat's
social standing.

**11–13**   As those present exit to leave the couple to have some 'private
speech' with each other, Giovanni (whose jealousy we know is acute)
takes the opportunity to remind Annabella not to be 'all woman'; in
other words, faithless. It is notable how he – without any evidence –
assumes that she, and indeed all women, are by nature fickle. The
exclamation on Soranzo's 'Vasques!' (12) suggests that in most situations, however private, he might stay close to his master and need
to be reminded to leave; with his knowledge of Hippolita's threat he
may now be even more protective.

**13–62**   Left alone with Annabella, Soranzo begins his courtship.
Maybe her father's instruction that Annabella should treat him
'nobly' (7) suggests that he knows how feisty his daughter can be, but
her energetic responses to his opening gambit may nevertheless take
Soranzo by surprise. The scene is further complicated at l. 18 by the
arrival of Giovanni to watch and over-hear their conversation (from
the upper level) and to interject his own responses, and the scene
provides an example of the complex staging made possible by the use
of the main stage and balcony in the original playhouse. It is a scene
laden with asides that express the sub-text of deception that underlies
these relationships until IV.iii when the truth begins to surface. Here,
everyone on stage is a deceiver. On the face of it, the scene shows a
young nobleman wooing a young, unmarried woman, watched by
her anguished lover who fears rejection. Seen from another perspective, however, we see an adulterer, potential murderer and hypocrite

(Soranzo) attempting to seduce an incestuous girl, no longer a virgin, watched by her lover who is also her brother.

The lines from 15 to 29 are shared, allowing the speed of the playing to match the wit of Annabella's language and Soranzo's attempts to get her to take him seriously, while the plethora of asides are used by Ford to reveal the characters' true feelings about the situation. When Soranzo eventually recognizes that she is making fun of him by taking his (conventional) language literally, she wins him round, as she did Donado, with a display of plain-speaking (43–50). At this point, however, (and the actress will need to consider exactly what prompts her to do so), she goes further, confirming that of all her suitors, if she were to choose one, it would be him, but she makes him promise not to tell her father she said it. Her rejection of him is complete enough to convince Giovanni of her commitment (57), and while Bergeron is right to note that 'Surely there has been ample of evidence of this during the several months of their incestuous love' (1986: 214), the line's main purpose is further to underline her brother's fundamental jealousy and doubt.

**62–71** At this moment, when all three suitors seem to have been successfully deflected, the crisis breaks, as Annabella is suddenly taken ill, though there has earlier been mention that she has been 'sickly' (II.i.55–6).

**72–end of scene** Soranzo seems not only reconciled to Annabella's answers, but genuinely concerned for her well-being, while Vasques (his quick aside at l. 79 confirming his earlier reluctance to leave) diagnoses 'the maid's sickness', a readiness for sexual activity, which in excess – 'an overflux of youth' – may prove dangerous, and require a 'present' (i.e. immediate) remedy: marriage.

*The question arises with this scene as to whether Annabella is aware of Giovanni's presence or not. My recollection of performances I have seen is that it is invariably played as if she is not, and there is clearly real value in a scene that shows Annabella operating alone, as it were, not via the male members of her family. But there is nothing in the text to confirm or challenge that reading. A workshop exercise with my students, playing the scene with both Annabella and Giovanni aware of each other, focused on the exchanges at 41–2. Rather than Annabella's sudden allusion to Soranzo as a 'looking glass' either being ignored (as in the Penguin, Revels, 1968 New Mermaids, Routledge and Oxford World's Classics editions) or explained, not entirely helpfully I think, as playing 'on the image of dressing one's hair at the mirror' (2003 New Mermaids edition), the actors were interested on why this line of all others should prompt Giovanni's, which significantly is tied to hers by completing it to make a full line: 'I'm confirmed.' It occurred to us that if Annabella is alert to her brother's presence, and only two scenes earlier had been made aware of how jealous he is of Soranzo, she might see this as an opportunity to set his mind at rest, and that might lead to her confidence in the 'promise' she can then make to Soranzo, which had also puzzled us. We thought it possible that her overt reference to Soranzo not being a mirror might be read by her brother as a direct recollection of Giovanni's description of their twinned nature as resembling reflections of each other, a concept given direct theatrical expression in the mirror image of their betrothal in I.ii. Of course, this is interpretation and therefore open to dispute, but even considering the scene in this way opened up new perspectives on the meanings of lines and also the complex dynamics of the asides.*

## Act III, scene iii

**1–end of scene** The distraught, anxious woman who enters with news that Annabella is pregnant is very different from the cool, confident and salaciously witty Putana who joked through the moments of sexual union that have produced the child. The tentative web of evasion that Annabella has spun by her deft dealings with her suitors is now, as Putana makes clear to Giovanni, irrevocably broken. Putana knows that this is not a case of a marriage being necessary, but a case of pregnancy being concealed, and Annabella's condition must be kept from a doctor at all costs if the fact is to be kept secret. Giovanni's final speech brilliantly captures his confusion, torn between concern for his sister's well-being and his fear of discovery. In a striking example of how performance can constantly illuminate a play in new ways, Jonathan Cullen (Giovanni in the 1991 RSC production; see pp. 116–19) did not recoil on hearing of Annabella's pregnancy, but jumping 'like toast ejecting from an overenthusiastic toaster' asked excitedly for details as any prospective father might, underlining his (tragically misplaced) conviction that the incestuous nature of the relationship is a problem only because of society's attitude to it (Lomax 1995: xix). The final speech is in verse, to contrast with the prose of the rest of the scene, and as it darts from one thing to another, embodies his exhilaration mixed with awareness of the potential danger of the situation they are now in.

*This marks the end of the second 'movement' of the play. There can be no hope now of the lovers keeping their relationship sealed off from the social world that surrounds them: 'The advent of Annabella's pregnancy acts as a touchstone for all of the play's moral attitudes and finds them all equally wanting' (McCabe 1993: 237).*

## Act III, scene iv

**1–23**  Just as we do not know the supposed manner of his death, nor do we know anything of Richardetto's life apart from the fact that he is not a doctor. However, presumably as he is close at hand, he finds himself being required to provide a diagnosis on Annabella. In a sense, this is as good as Putana's hope that she not be seen by any doctor, as Richardetto, while he discounts Annabella's explanation that she's suffering from eating melons, attributes her condition – as Vasques did earlier – to sexual ripeness. (The New Mermaid editor Martin Wiggins (2003) ponders whether Richardetto does, in fact, recognize that she is pregnant but conceals that in order to see Soranzo married to a woman who is not a virgin, but there is no other suggestion that this is in his mind and it seems that his medical incompetence is what saves them.) The most pressing matter is to get Annabella married as soon as possible, so the Friar is to be sent for immediately. Richardetto plays no further part in the scene. It is possible he exits at l. 26 (though there are no other unmarked exits or entrances in the first printed edition) or that he simply withdraws and observes the exchanges that follow. I favour the first option, as it helps explain why, in III.v, he tells Grimaldi that the imminent betrothal, even the marriage, will take place in the Friar's cell whereas we know that the Friar has arrived at Florio's house.

**23–end of scene**  The Friar, entering with Giovanni, greets Florio on a half-line, maintaining the speed of action in the scene and act as a whole. Giovanni expresses concern for his sister's soul, but Florio knows that Annabella is unlikely to die, and believes the Friar's arrival hastens the possibility of a marriage: his daughter will listen to him. Florio's line (35) can be interpreted in a number of ways: 'impression' might simply mean 'idea', 'dear impression' could be Annabella herself, but the word could also carry the sense of an 'imprinted likeness'. Roper suggests a paraphrase: 'I bear the imprinted likeness of my own dear father, and before I die I should wish to see my own child married (and ready to transmit the likeness to another generation)', further underlining the importance of inheritance.

## Act III, scene v

**1–7**   The action now shifts from the flurry of action in Florio's home to the measured rhythm of Grimaldi's plans for revenge on Soranzo. His short soliloquy, spoken directly to the audience, offers some explanation why, having placed so much emphasis on his 'honour', he is now prepared to use underhand tactics to prevent Soranzo's marriage.

**8–21**   Richardetto brings the poison and gives Grimaldi what we know to be possibly erroneous information about Soranzo's movements. Their shared loathing of Soranzo and sense that his death is not far off prompts the warmth of their parting.

**22–5**   Perhaps they have embraced, the action prompting Richardetto to confess in a short soliloquy that if successful he will even 'hug revenge', as he imagines the wedding feast turned into a funeral wake. But there are other matters in hand, too.

**26–34**   Encouraged by her uncle, Philotis has managed to find a way to love Bergetto (a contrast with the less pliable Annabella). Bergetto, however, is keen to marry her as quickly as possible in case his uncle, Donado, intervenes to prevent it (though given what we know he thinks of his nephew it is hard to think why; perhaps Bergetto is wise enough to think a doctor's niece might not bring the sought-after dowry). Richardetto is keen to help bring this about and suggests they should go to the Friar's (earlier than he believes Soranzo to be going there with Annabella), and in disguise in case they are spotted and Donado alerted to their plans. We might, as an audience, sense that this heavy plotting has more than just a narrative purpose, but not be aware of what particular purpose it may be put to.

**35–end of scene**   Bergetto and Poggio arrive. Bergetto is amorous, excited at the prospect of marriage, but Richardetto knows there are plans to be made. Crucially, after he kisses her, Philotis's one line in the scene suggests that while she might have pursued marriage with Bergetto at her uncle's behest, Bergetto's kiss and obvious affection for her might promise a satisfying relationship.

## Act III, scene vi

0 *Enter the* **FRIAR** *in his study, sitting in a chair,* **ANNABELLA** *kneeling and whispering to him, a table before them and wax lights; she weeps, and wrings her hands.* As we have already seen in this play, and as one finds in his others, Ford's words are given great emotional force by the visual effects he so carefully creates. Exactly where the scene is set, however, is important. The indication that it is the Friar's study, presumably his cell, seems to be contradicted by the reference at l. 45 to Soranzo waiting downstairs. If, however, the scene takes place in Annabella's chamber, which seems to follow from earlier statements, that changes the original plan in III.iv for the betrothal to take place away from Florio's house.

1–23 Annabella finds herself in a position similar to Giovanni at the start of the play, though her mental and emotional state is very different: pregnant, alone, frightened, distraught and much less able than her brother – driven by his unshakable certainty in himself – to withstand the Friar. He is the only person other than Putana who knows exactly what the situation is, and having failed to have any effect on Giovanni, this is his opportunity to persuade Annabella to bring her relationship with her brother to an end. This is the moment, so far in the play, where the greatest pressure is brought to bear on her. His tactic is basically to frighten her, his description that she has 'unripped a soul' reminding us of Giovanni's injunction that she should 'rip up' his bosom if she needs to see his heart, the emblem and proof of his love for her (I.ii.205). In Chapter 3 I discuss how Ford draws on other writers' work, but here he draws on his own: the Friar's description of the hell to which Annabella will go if she refuses to repent is based closely on Ford's poem *Christ's Bloody Sweat* (see p. 156). The Friar's examples are similar to those visions Giovanni dismissed in I.ii as 'dreams and old men's tales' designed to 'fright unsteady youth' (152–3), rather than steadfast lovers such as he.

24–43 Now the Friar moves from the general – examples of those who have illicit sexual relationships – to the particular, and for the first time in the play uses the word 'incest' which, up to this point, has been the hidden, unspoken centre in Giovanni's exchanges with his sister, concealed beneath his manipulation, his willful distortion of the ideals of his professed Platonic beliefs. Bonaventura (using the image of each kiss from her brother as being like a 'dagger's point', specifically recalling Giovanni's dagger in I.ii) shifts the blame directly on to Annabella as he paints a picture of even Giovanni wishing his sister had never given in to her desire for him when 'she did yield to lust' (30). Throughout, Annabella has been crying, a sign the Friar interprets as showing her willingness to seek redemption. And as she turns to him for help, he sees the opportunity to achieve what Giovanni rejected earlier: to get her married to Soranzo and not to wait a moment longer, but 'take the time' (seize the present moment). It is not the first time the Friar has shifted from a moral argument to a frankly pragmatic one, here to solve the overriding necessity to conceal her pregnancy; saving her soul must take second place to sham respectability. And though the Friar recognizes that 'the baits of sin / Are hard to leave' (i.e. her love for her brother), he clearly believes her repentance will overcome those temptations. Is Annabella's repentance genuine? Or is she responding to the pressure she is under? Unlike at the beginning of V.i the play at this point does not provide an answer, but the actor playing Annabella will need to be clear. (See Findlay 1999: 28–9, Strout 1990: 173 and Woods 2010 for views on this question.)

*Looking back at this scene once we know how the play ends, we may register the way it prefigures that climax: the Friar's description of her soul being 'unripped', his predictions that her brother's kisses will seem like 'daggers' points', and the reference to the 'new motions' of her 'heart'. Later in the play, the repetition of 'rip' will strike us again, as first Soranzo threatens to 'rip up' Annabella's bosom, this time to find the secret name her heart conceals, and finally, when Giovanni insanely triumphs that he has 'ripped' out his sister's heart.*

**44–8** Florio and Giovanni have obviously been waiting close by, and enter immediately the Friar calls for them, the scene gathering speed with the short, shared lines between the characters. While the Friar has been working on Annabella, Soranzo has been sent for, has arrived and been informed of what is planned. As Giovanni leaves to get Soranzo, his aside to the audience expresses his fears that his sister has succumbed to the Friar.

**48–end of scene**  A climactic moment, as Giovanni watches his sister join hands with Soranzo, known at the time as a 'handfasting' and, in effect, a formal confirmation of the couple's betrothal. It is, in miniature, an echo of III.ii. Vasques is a silent observer, so it will be up to the actor to show any doubts he may have about this outcome.

## Act III, scene vii

**1–3**  Grimaldi enters carrying a 'dark lantern' – that is, one with a device for obscuring its light without extinguishing it. His opening lines are obviously addressed to the audience.

**4–14**  Bergetto and Philotis enter, with Richardetto and Poggio some distance behind; perhaps they do not actually enter until Grimaldi has finished his lines. Grimaldi calls to 'some angry Justice' to guide his hand, which Ford's audience would interpret as a call to Providence for aid, but he nevertheless kills the wrong man. It is important that none of the other characters sees Grimaldi actually stab Bergetto and exit, and that Bergetto himself has no idea exactly what has happened to him. This is perfectly feasible: an article in the *Guardian* (('Blooding of the New Blades', 28 December 1992) on street violence explained that young men stabbed in the chest or the back are often unaware of the seriousness of their injuries until they reach the hospital.

**15–26**  Richardetto dispatches Poggio for help and lights, back the way they have just come from, before he moves to Bergetto, his doubt over the extent of Bergetto's injuries resulting from the fact that neither he – nor the audience – can see very well (the 1991 RSC production played the scene in virtually total darkness). Getting the shift of tones and mood of the scene is crucial. Bergetto, presented from the outset as a buffoon is still, from the point of view of his companions, playing the fool, and it is vital that the actor's performance – especially in the moments up to the stabbing, when he is perhaps larking about – allows this interpretation to be placed upon it. It is not until Poggio returns accompanied by Officers with lights, and a torch or lantern is either passed to Richardetto or held near him, that the truth of the situation suddenly dawns on them.

**27–end of scene** Following the exit of the Officers (the departure of their lanterns again darkening the stage) the mood switches once more, and the rapidity with which the tone changes from one extreme to another, from laughter (which may also be raised by the Officers' exit unless care is taken) to sympathy to sorrow, all within the space of only 38 lines, is characteristic of much Jacobean drama (White, 1998: 177–96). The sense of disruption and confusion is aided by the constant shifting of the light as the characters (and audience) try to work out what's going on. Philotis starts to tear her petticoat to make bandages, while Richardetto comforts Bergetto. Bergetto has appeared in six out of the 16 scenes up to this point and has figured prominently in each. Anderson dismisses the character as merely a 'comical booby', who proves 'more tiresome than funny and does not serve as an effective parallel or foil to either Giovanni or Soranzo' (1972: 105), but performances have successfully overturned that assertion, and in a play rife with selfish and self-seeking men, especially in their attitudes to women, the poignancy of this innocent's death is underlined by his concern for Philotis. The final image (Richardetto perhaps having led Philotis away) of Poggio cradling his dead friend is a deeply moving one, the more so because of its contrast with the mood of the earlier part of the scene.

*This scene, with the unexpected, accidental death of Bergetto draws clear comparisons with the death of Mercutio in* Romeo and Juliet *(III.i) on which it is obviously based, and in both plays the death and removal of the principal 'comic' character marks a tipping point and signals the ultimately tragic outcome of the play. Here, too, we witness a revenge plot rebounding on an innocent victim and may wonder what impact that might have on the perpetrators.*

## Act III, scene viii

A short scene between Vasques and Hippolita, its function is to act as a kind of commentary on other plot lines to keep them alive (most importantly the plot against Soranzo) while the death of Bergetto strand of the narrative is played out.

## Act III, scene ix

**1–9**  At the same time as Donado weeps for his murdered nephew, a brusque and pragmatic Florio urges him to seek justice, while Richardetto's pious hypocrisy and mealy-mouthed attempt to cover his tracks by accepting that he was in part responsible will harden our attitude towards this enigmatic and devious man.

**10–28**  Under questioning, the Officers are able to identify the attacker precisely (they know him as a suitor to Annabella) and saw him let into the Cardinal's palace, but were not prepared to pursue him inside. Richardetto is presumably uneasy at this turn of events: openly he assures the others that the Cardinal will mete out justice, but he must be concerned that Grimaldi might reveal Richardetto's part in the plot.

**29–61 *Enter* CARDINAL *and* GRIMALDI**  Cardinals in early modern English plays are invariably presented as corrupt and self-seeking. With Grimaldi (from whom he has learned of Bergetto's death) brazenly standing by his side, the Cardinal's acknowledgement of the social status of Florio and Donado as 'masters of the common-wealth' underlines the disdain with which he nevertheless treats them. Kneeling to the Cardinal, Grimaldi confesses to the crime (without mentioning Richardetto's role) but – shamelessly claiming that he was provoked by Soranzo's refusal to fight him – argues that his revenge on Soranzo would have been justifiable and by implication he can't be held responsible for not killing the person he meant to kill, and he throws himself on the Cardinal's mercy. Given what we have seen of the Cardinal we will not be astonished (and no doubt many in Ford's audience would have been even less surprised) that Grimaldi's admission is enough to lead the Cardinal to take him into the protection of the Pope. Nor, having already expressed his dislike of them, can the Cardinal resist a specific jibe at Florio for having rejected the 'nobly born' Grimaldi as 'too mean' a husband for his daughter. The clipped tones of his final, insulting lines draw the interview to a close.

**62–end of act**  Left dazed by this display of corruption, when 'cardinals think murder's not amiss', Florio is right in his judgement that 'Justice is fled to heaven'. The city of Parma is an even more corrupt environment than they had imagined, but the reality is, as Florio points out, that 'Great men' (like the Cardinal and Soranzo) 'may do their wills, we must obey'.

*The overall impression of Act III is of speed. Although in total lines (407) the act is roughly comparable with all but Act II, it contains nine scenes, a third of all the scenes in the play, and each scene is short (the first scene is the shortest with 23, the second, with 84 lines, the longest). Right from the start of the act there is a sense in all the characters of the need for haste. Poggio tells the newly enamoured Bergetto to 'Lose no time then' (III.i.20) in marrying Philotis; Florio's insistence in III.ii that Soranzo must be seriously considered as a potential husband puts increased pressure on Annabella, while her collapse at the end of the scene panics everyone, Giovanni in particular, and leads Florio to demand her marriage 'within these few days' and then, a few lines later, 'now' (III.iv.10, 19), while Ford puns on the meanings of 'speed' (haste/success). The Friar wants Annabella to 'weep faster' (III.vi.5) and seizes the opportunity to press on with the marriage to Soranzo. III.vii is a scene of confusion as help is desperately sought for the dying Bergetto, and concludes with a promise to find the murderer quickly; in III.viii Hippolita wants two days shrunk to two hours; and as the act concludes, Florio understands that Justice itself has promptly fled the city of Parma.*

# Act IV

## Act IV, scene i

**0  A banquet. Hautbonys. Enter the FRIAR, GIOVANNI, ANNABELLA, PHILOTIS, SORANZO, DONADO, FLORIO, RICHARDETTO, PUTANA and VASQUES.**  Another detailed stage direction, here for a banquet, the second to take place, but the first to be seen (the first takes place off-stage in I.ii). The setting is accompanied by hautboys (an early form of oboe, though the word could also apply to the player of the instrument). Of 99 extant plays written between 1585 and 1642, 114 include scenes for which the setting is a banquet, and a link emerged early in that period between banquets and the consummation of a revenge plot (Meads 2001: 1–2).

**1–14**  The scene opens with the Friar's enthusiastic (and no doubt relieved) welcome to the guests now the marriage is actually concluded, and hopes that the couple's joy may be long lasting. (The RSC 1977 production began with an interpolated wedding ceremony, in Latin, led by the Friar; see pp. 112–13.) Soranzo shamelessly interprets his escape from the failed attack by Grimaldi that led to Bergetto's murder (III.vii) as an intervention of 'the hand of goodness' (i.e. god). The audience, however, will also recall Hippolita's pledge to Vasques that she will send Soranzo 'to his last and lasting sleep' on his wedding day (III.viii.4), and know that he is not out of danger.

**15–28**  Soranzo's joy (or triumph) is evidently not shared by his bride nor by Giovanni, who is forced to express his private thoughts in an aside. As often with Giovanni, his words are extravagant, and his consequent demeanour sufficiently expressive (we have seen him externalize his emotions in I.ii), to prompt Vasques (a keen observer) to ask after his well-being. Although these two have not spoken before in the play the mere fact that Vasques is Soranzo's servant is enough for Giovanni to respond aggressively. No reaction from Vasques is indicated, but presumably he notes the vehemence of Giovanni's retort, and ponders on its cause. The moment between them is truncated by Soranzo calling for a toast, drinking from the 'weighty bowl' before offering it to Giovanni. (The earlier reference at l. 14 to 'cups' is slightly confusing, but it refers to the 'toasts' rather than the vessels they are drunk from.) Giovanni refuses, his use of 'offend' carrying both the sense of 'cause me some physical discomfort' but also, for the audience the revulsion he feels towards Soranzo and the whole situation. Annabella reads both meanings, and attempts to defuse the moment, but at that instant the noise of new arrivals is heard off-stage.

**29–35**  If, to an early modern audience, a banquet might signal possible mayhem, the announcement (from Vasques, no less) of a masque (or entertainment) to accompany the feast, would add an even greater frisson. We should note, however, the powerful dramatic emblem the masque provided. Although most commonly an entertainment staged within the royal court as a theatrical expression of the monarch's virtues and power, masques were also presented in the large houses of wealthy aristocrats like Soranzo, and often at times of particular celebration such as a marriage. Moreover, the masque carries forward the notion of self-conscious performance that emerges increasingly strongly in the play, as here Hippolita stages herself as the rejected woman. As the hautboys play their reedy music, Hippolita and her fellow performers, all masked, enter and dance. Their white robes symbolize purity, while their garlands of willow are emblems of grief for unrequited love. In Ford's day, brides wore their best, or specially made clothes, but not white. In modern productions, however, Annabella is also invariably dressed in a white bridal-gown (taking the hint from her reference to her 'gay attires', V.v.20), which makes a powerful connection with Hippolita.

**36–84**   The surprise that everyone, especially Soranzo, expresses as Hippolita unmasks herself is sustained as she starts to speak. Turning first to Soranzo, and in measured, reasonable language – very different from her passionate outbursts the last time we saw them together – she sets out their past, arguing that though rumour has surrounded their relationship, the gossip will eventually peter out. Then, addressing Annabella, she reassures her that despite what has passed between Soranzo and herself, she has no intention of making any claim on him. Indeed, she takes Soranzo's hand and joins it with Annabella's, a symbolic act that mirrors the marriage they have just celebrated. Soranzo, no doubt surprised at this unexpected turn of events, especially in the light of their last rancorous meeting, can do no more than acknowledge his debt to her. But Hippolita is not finished: she renounces all vows made between them (and which she spelled out in detail in II.ii) and proposes her own toast to seal their new-found amity. As we no doubt recall her malice towards Soranzo in II.ii and her determination in III.viii to murder him, we may ourselves now be bemused by this turn of events, but only if the actress playing Hippolita is careful to give us no clue as to whether she speaks from the heart or not. Indeed, it is only her aside to Vasques at l. 61 that jolts us back to the 'plot' between them, though it is not until Vasques prevents Soranzo from drinking that we realize exactly what that plot was, and that Hippolita has made a fatal error by misjudging Vasques and over-estimating her own powers of seduction. As the poison takes effect, and she and Vasques trade insults, the guests can only wonder what on earth is going on, until Vasques offers them a detailed explanation. (The two long dashes in l. 82 in the 1633 quarto may indicate that the compositor could not read what was written in the manuscript, or may have been where words were crossed out in the manuscript but no replacement given. In production it might be appropriate to add something like 'She hath yet minutes to live', which Hippolita picks up at l. 87.)

**85–6**   If the wedding guests' responses signal sympathy only for Soranzo, Richardetto's reveals a relief, perhaps, that his revenge has been enacted by heaven and so taken off his hands – and conscience – though Vasques would seem more the helpmate of the devil. To us, it may be Richardetto who appears self-righteous, and hypocritical.

**86–104**   Completing Richardetto's line (though not recognizing that her husband's mask is still firmly in place), Hippolita might appear at first to share his view of the justice of her end. It seems, however, that she is confirming Vasques's prediction of the nearness of her death, and she seizes her last opportunity to curse Soranzo and his marriage. Her death is greeted by more pious observations, and that they will almost inevitably seem trite to us is because the play has complicated our responses beyond these simple statements. The wedding feast is drawn to a hasty close.

**105–end of scene**   As Hippolita's body is carried off, the Friar has the last words of the scene, just as he had the first. His tone is very different, however, from the determined buoyancy of his opening lines when he spoke openly to all present. Now his words must be cloaked in the verbal mask of an aside: Hippolita and Richardetto are not the only ones concealing their true natures and feelings. Hippolita is probably carried off by Vasques (as the only servant present, but more likely because he has managed her death), and if he does it would present an ironic visual image of a groom bearing his bride across the threshold. I suspect that the body is moved as soon as Donado gives the instruction (l. 104), possibly with everyone else exiting at the same time so that the Friar's thrillingly ominous lines to Giovanni that close the scene are not lost in the mass exit. However, in performance his closing couplet may get a laugh (which a production should not try to prevent) from an audience sharp enough to pick up, and react to, the notion that marriages are *seldom* (but therefore are *sometimes*) happy and successful after such a disastrous wedding day.

   *The scene began with images of heaven, an event 'pleasing to the saints' who, unseen, observe the wedding. It ends with an image of hell, as Hippolita's* poisoned body burns with a 'Heat above hell fire' (l. 89). In a sense the scene encapsulates the world of the play as a whole: a respectable, pious surface, but a seething underbelly of deception, corruption and revenge. Annabella speaks only two lines in the scene, the first to try to protect her brother from Soranzo's exuberance (l. 28), the second to express her horror at the body of Hippolita, contorted in death (l. 99). We need to remember these two tensions in her life: love for her brother, on one side, and, on the other, the religious and social sanctions – and punishments – that may follow.

## Act IV, scene ii

**1–21**　Philotis has been a silent observer of the violence of the previous scene, the second death she's witnessed in a very short space of time. Something needs to be done to show that this scene, however, is not a direct follow on from IV.i, as there has been enough time since the wedding for there to be 'much talk' about how badly the marriage is going. Indeed, the confidence that Richardetto expressed, following Hippolita's death, that her fate was heaven's work, is now extended to his belief that God has intervened directly in Soranzo's marriage and that 'No life is blessed but the way to heaven'. In relinquishing his own role as an avenger on Soranzo to the 'the one above' (following the biblical injunction, 'avenge not yourselves… Vengeance is mine, I will repay, saith the Lord', *Romans*, 12–19) he takes a course of action similar to that imposed on Charlemont by the ghost of his murdered father in *The Atheist's Tragedy* (1611), to 'Attend with patience the success of things / But leave revenge unto the King of kings' (II. vi.22–3). Whether because Philotis is no longer of direct use to him, or because he genuinely fears for her in the 'hazard of these woes' (l. 16), he imitates Hamlet's advice to Ophelia and proposes she should seek refuge in a nunnery, and renounce a world that displays such immorality. However, if we recall Theseus's description of a nun's life in *A Midsummer Night's Dream* as 'in shady cloister to be mewed, / To live a barren sister all your life' (I.i.71–2), added to the later image of Annabella 'mewed up in a cage / Unmated' (V.i.14–15) it will underline the extent to which both women's freedom of action is constrained and curtailed by men.

**22–end of scene**　The fact that Philotis asks her uncle to repeat his proposal, and her response to his repetition of it, might suggest that the sudden shift from near-wife to celibate nun is not a course of action she welcomes. The scene concludes with three sets of rhyming couplets, and these, especially the almost stock nature of her final couplet, at odds with the complex moralities that drive the play as a whole, might give the actress playing Philotis cause to reflect on what the character might actually intend to do once she is safely away from Parma and her domineering uncle.

*The sub-plots in this play are frequently dismissed by critics (see p. 114), though discussion focuses largely on their content and language and rarely includes consideration of their position in the play. As Alan Dessen observes, if a reader or spectator is interested only in Giovanni and Annabella, then IV.ii may seem like 'a final dose of sub-plot to be endured before the main event'. Yet by examining the decision in a production at the Oregon Shakespearean Festival in 1981 to re-order the scenes to run III.ix, IV.i, interval, IV.iii, IV.ii, Dessen points out that making the scene between Richardetto and Philotis follow IV. iii means the characters' choices mean something quite different, and so changes 'radically the meaning and function of the sequence as a whole' (1986: 97).*

## Act IV, scene iii

**o** *Enter* **SORANZO**, *unbraced, and* **ANNABELLA** *dragged in.* Ford's audience, watching this, may well have recalled the image of Hamlet, in a state of turmoil, 'unbraced' (II.i.78), or the equally brutal opening to IV.iii of Chapman's still-popular play *Bussy d'Ambois*, where a cuckolded husband confronts his adulterous wife: '*MONTSURRY, bare, unbraced, pulling TAMYRA in by the hair, FRIAR. One bearing light, a standish* [a stand for pen and ink] *and paper, which sets a table.*' (See Ide, 1986: 78–9 for further parallels between Chapman's and Ford's plays.)

**1–14** Soranzo's state of undress, and the violence of his physical and verbal behaviour towards Annabella, emphatically underlined by the sword he brandishes (l. 3; an echo of the dagger that figured in her 'betrothal' to her brother in I.ii), effect a telling contrast with the language and action at the opening of II.i when Giovanni and Annabella entered 'as from their chamber'. Picking up on the image of the mask that pervaded the previous scene, Soranzo (aware now that his bride was not a virgin) casts himself as the bawd (brothel keeper) who pays for his wife's upkeep, as a pimp supports a prostitute, for other men's sexual use. His attack draws on a range of traditional misogynistic complaints against women – their inconstancy, their lechery, their deceitfulness – though his tone of righteous indignation will be strongly tempered for us by our knowledge of his own past behaviour. It is also significant (and in line with the male-dominated morality of Parma) that Soranzo's rage is driven more by the affront to his masculine pride, by the fact that his disgrace may be publicly known, than that his wife has betrayed him. He also now knows that she is pregnant, and that he must be the 'dad' to the bastard ('gallimaufry') she carries. The seemingly modern word 'dad', though common in Ford's day, may strike us as oddly informal in the context of the speech. 'Gallimaufry', a word which may sound as strange as 'dad' does familiar, carried a range of meanings for Ford's audience, all circling in some way around the idea of hodge-podge, a mix of different stuffs. However, looking back to the banquet in IV.i and forward to the banquet in V.v, and at Giovanni's imagery in particular, the association of 'gallimaufry' with food, a dish made up of odds and ends of food, needs to be kept in mind.

**15–27**  The scene from this point until the entrance of the prose-speaking Vasques is replete with shared lines, driving the row between them forward with great energy. Annabella's retort – 'Beastly man' – may sound tame to our ears, but to a Jacobean it was more forceful, a charge that Soranzo resembles an animal in unintelligence, in being brutish and cruel, and with connotations (obsolete now) of cowardice and being unmanly. More striking, however, is the difference in Annabella, a contrast made even more forceful following her near-silence the last time we saw her, in IV.i. I noted the haste of decision and activity in the third act and here Annabella lays part of the blame on Soranzo's eagerness to marry: given time, she claims, she would have told him what condition she was in. Punctuated with his insults ('quean', meaning prostitute, and pronounced like 'queen', is a common pun) she pushes on forcefully, not evading but expanding on the situation: that she only married him for honour, that if he could find it in himself to accept the situation stoically she might even in time come to love him, and that she has freely confessed she is pregnant.

**28–34**  There is one thing she will not do, however: reveal the identity of the father. But, unable, it seems, to stop herself, and recognizing the strength of Soranzo's desire to know who it is, she embarks on a panegyric about the father, and, she is certain, the son she is carrying. The phrase 'your longing stomach', is a complex one: its surface meaning is 'to satisfy your craving for the name', but beneath that is a reference to the 'longing' some women experience in pregnancy for normally unpalatable things and, even perhaps, an echo of Vasques's insulting remark to Grimaldi that he should take warm broth to 'stay [his] stomach' (I.ii.48), in other words to satisfy his appetite or calm his aggression.

**34–42** Soranzo's rebuke prompts her to stop, but urged on by Soranzo, and accepting the bargain that he will kill her for doing so, she continues her praises for her lover, casting him (as she did when she spied him in I.ii) as a celestial, even spiritual figure, whose beauty would overpower a woman who was more than human, let alone a mere mortal like herself, while taunting Soranzo that, if he will not worship this man, he is unfit to kneel before him. Alison Findlay interprets this as Annabella reconciling the conflicting roles demanded of her by the men 'through identification with the Virgin Mary, the second Eve whose sexual experience is God-given and for whom motherhood is a source of redemption, not the result of damnation', and, by extension of the analogy, 'casting Giovanni in the role of God' and consigning Soranzo to play 'the part of a doubtful Joseph' (1999: 29–30). This is not only a truly daring argument for Annabella to make (and probably one an audience now will not follow in the heat of performance) but a blasphemous one that, briefly, allows her to find a justification for breaking all conventional moral codes. However, we may also recall Giovanni's own reference to a mortal woman finding sexual pleasure with a god, in his early analogy of Leda and the swan, that image of unnatural lust (II.i.16–17).

**43–55** Soranzo wants the name of this matchless lover; without that how can he dispatch Vasques to kill him? But still Annabella delays. Indeed, the scene has something akin to a sexual tension, as Soranzo begs for relief while she holds out. The best she can offer is that Soranzo will have a chance to play the role of father to the son she bears. Indeed, she turns the knife again, pointing out that had she not been forced to marry him, as far as she is concerned, Soranzo might as well never have existed. Increasingly enraged, but with really only one thing on his mind, Soranzo once more demands the man's name, only to be rebuffed again, the lightness of Annabella's deflections only serving to wind him up still more, as his threats become more violent and more 'beastly' (l. 1): threatening to rip up her heart and when he discovers who it is, tear him to pieces with his teeth ('prodigious' meaning monstrous, or unnatural).

**56–63** The scene now moves into a different register as Annabella first laughs (prompting Soranzo to even more violent threats against her body) then starts to sing, in Italian. His astonishment at her open derision for his attempts to intimidate her is captured in his sequence of questions ('Dost thou laugh?… Dost thou triumph?… Dost thou not tremble yet?'). Her singing marks a breaking point for Soranzo, and the repetition of 'thus' (l. 60) indicates that he moves from verbal threats (though 'lust-belepered' – not Ford's coining; it was used in a play a few years before his – shows no diminution of those) to physical violence, pulling her hair and dragging her again across the stage.

**64–76** Unable to control Annabella or make her confess, Soranzo makes an even stronger threat to kill her. Again she welcomes the possibility. Her comparison of him to a hangman may suggest he has her in some kind of strangle-hold on her (though obviously the actor can still breathe and speak at the rate this passionate scene demands), and also acts as yet another insult against his honour (similar to the way Vasques treats Grimaldi in I.ii), as the job of hangman was considered a base one, and far beneath the dignity of an aristocrat like Soranzo. However, while daring him to kill her, she also threatens him with the revenge that will be taken on him by the yet-unnamed lover. As he prepares to kill her, he asks if Florio knows the truth, presumably intending to torture it out of her father if necessary. He gives her one last chance to reveal the name, which she defiantly rejects, and he emphasizes that he will not cease his revenge on her lover after her death.

*We may have thought the revenge plots had burned themselves out with the failed attempt on Soranzo and the death of Hippolita, but with Soranzo's discovery of Annabella's pregnancy we are once more plunged into a cycle of revenge and, we must assume, counter-revenge.*

**77–105**  Soranzo is clearly about to kill her when he is prevented by the arrival of Vasques, the shared line suggesting the interruption. It seems likely that Vasques in some way pulls him away, given Soranzo's order to his servant to 'forbear' (in this context meaning 'keep back', 'don't interfere'). Having seen Vasques in action with Hippolita in II.ii and III.viii, and the consequences of his 'performance' of friendship to her in IV.i, we will be especially alert to his tactics in this situation. Has Vasques overheard the row between them? He seems aware of the 'faults' committed by Annabella, and it doesn't seem plausible that Soranzo's description of her as a 'damned whore' would be sufficient in itself. Nevertheless (in prose as always), he moves instantly to an eloquent defence of her. In some senses he follows a line similar to Putana's easy morality in I.ii.74–98, but he also argues that it is not reasonable to demand to know the lover's name: indeed, he adds (in a move seemingly designed to appeal to his master's sense of honour), it is rather a sign of her 'worth' that she refuses to disclose it, and indeed that she refuses to beg for her own life. His aside to Soranzo (98–100) reveals his true purpose to him, and to us, as he prompts Soranzo to leave the detective work to him, before he returns to his theme of persuading his master of the manly, indeed godly, virtues of stoically enduring and even forgiving the wrongs done to him.

**106–16**  Soranzo seems to take his instructions well. In verse, he once more rebukes Annabella for betraying him, but now in tones of sorrow not anger. Vasques (in an aside, rather like a director's notes to an actor) compliments him on this tempered performance, but now asks him to increase the level of emotion, to let Annabella see how deeply these events have affected him.

**117–46**  Under Vasques's direction, Soranzo is revealing himself to be a skilled actor. Focusing strongly on Annabella, he draws from her a confession that she knew he loved her, which he underlines by arguing that her lover may have been attracted by her outward beauty, but that he loved her heart and her virtue. The scene is moving rapidly between extremes of energy and emotion, and it is crucial that Soranzo's words and behaviour as a man whose rage is 'overpassed' justify not only Annabella's response, but Vasques's too, otherwise the scene risks becoming melodramatic. Soranzo now moves a step further, invoking the view held by many in Ford's day that, as expressed in the Bible, wives should 'submit yourselves unto your own husbands, as unto the Lord. For the husband is the head of the wife, even as Christ is the head of the church' (*Ephesians*, 5:22–3). In other words, Soranzo is offering – if Annabella will be true to him from this point – to pardon her previous faults, and take her as his wife. Vasques quickly points out how generous that is, but there is no need, as Annabella, clearly affected deeply by his words, kneels before him (again note the play's recurrent motif of kneeling, each time in a different context). Before she can speak, however, Soranzo (perhaps knowing he cannot sustain this particular role of the forgiving husband much longer) sends her to her chamber (he has to repeat it so maybe she is reluctant to leave) where he will join her shortly.

**147–62** Vasques's confidence in the way he steers his master's behaviour is striking, as is the sarcasm of his reference to Soranzo's mood and language in IV.i. Soranzo is fired up but, as Vasques points out, he has no idea of how, or on whom, his revenge is to be carried out. His lines here are dense with complex and – to our ears – largely incomprehensible word-play, although the overlying tone and energy of what he says will probably be clear. In this situation, an actor might decide to put lines 151–5 into his own words to be sure he has the sense absolutely clear and a main task here is to recognize the various meanings of 'stock'. A paraphrase might go something like this: 'Alas, it is not uncommon these days for a man to marry a great/ pregnant woman, who has been handed over to you [in marriage; the significance of taking each other's hands, see IV.i.46] with her body [stock] already carrying the child that will carry on your line of descent [stock], just as a stem has a graft inserted into it [stock]. But the really skilful [cunning] task is to discover who the ferret was who hung about your bride's rabbit-burrow/vagina ['cony' also carried the sense of the dupe, conned by the cony-catcher].' Of course, the actor still has to *say* Ford's words. The problem will be how to catch the extreme vulgarity of Vasques's language and crucially the attitude to women it exposes, especially given his ability to charm women with his attitude of careful listening and sympathetic understanding. Ford's friend, Philip Massinger, describes the wives of poultry-sellers shouting 'No money, no cony' which catches the full vulgarity of Vasques's description of Annabella. Indeed, the abrupt way Vasques interrupts Soranzo (who does not appear to have been listening), the manner in which he instructs his master to go to Annabella, and Soranzo's acceptance of Vasques's proposal over his own, suggests almost a reversal of their roles and status. Soranzo leaves.

**163–72**  In the first line of this soliloquy it isn't clear whether Vasques is referring to the departing Soranzo or himself. 'Sirrah' is a term of address commonly addressed to a social inferior, and if aimed at Soranzo might enforce Vasques's own notion of his actual status in this relationship. He gives us a brief insight to the marital discord that has resulted from Annabella's behaviour, before embellishing his ideas with another complex analogy. He is aware that her swelling belly must have been concealed 'cunningly' by the dress-maker. His next line shows a rapid linking of word-meanings: 'Up' means pregnant; 'quick' means 'pregnant' and 'with speed', picked up in 'quickly'. But the real trick (a contemporary meaning of 'policy') will be to discover *who* the father is.

**173–202**  The sight of Putana, weeping, provides him with a way towards this discovery, and, consummate performer that he is, Vasques straight away switches from talking to the audience to seamlessly adopt the consoling, understanding tone we saw him employ with Hippolita. He immediately distances himself from Soranzo's anger, confirming that she is not alone in being mistreated by him, sympathizing with Annabella and, most important, hinting that if there were others who thought like him, Soranzo might find his life in danger. Vasques's tactic, as in his carefully measured verbal attack on Grimaldi (I.ii) and his persuasive behaviour with Hippolita (II. ii) and Annabella (IV.iii), is to suggest that it is the withholding of information that angers Soranzo, not the information itself, and that once he knows the identity of the father he will be placated. Putana's interest in this is encouraged by a veiled threat of Soranzo's planned, but deferred, violence towards her, which prompts her to admit she does know something. His next move is to flatter her, to acknowledge how Annabella in turn loves and trusts her, and to agree with Putana that she should keep faith with her charge. *But* – and this is a key moment in each of his strategic conversations – he assures her that in this instance, revealing this particular piece of information can only have beneficial results for Annabella, and for Putana too.

**203–22**   The breach in Putana's defences has been made, but Vasques knows better than to launch a direct attack, preferring a more oblique approach, allowing Putana, comforted by his reassurances, to at last offer to give him the information he wants. The punctuation mark '?' found at the end of l. 211 in the 1633 quarto can be modernized as either a question mark – which would maintain the gentle tone of his questioning – or as an exclamation mark – which would capture the idea that even Vasques did not expect this outcome: the performers will need to make a clear choice. Relieved of the burden of secrecy, Putana offers more than she has been asked to do: that Annabella and Giovanni's love affair – romanticized in her description of the 'brave gentleman' and 'fair lady' – continues 'perpetually', which carries the sense both of 'without interruption' (by Annabella's marriage) but also suggests that they have no intention of ending it. This knowledge is of particular value to Soranzo, especially as Putana (her tongue now fully loosened) confirms that the lovers will not be able to stay apart for long. She responds to his question with one, last vigorous assertion of her truthfulness, at which point, convinced, Vasques summons his 'banditti' (who have conveniently been waiting outside).

**223–32**   A characteristic of Jacobean plays is the speed with which they shift in mood, tone and rhythm, and Ford concludes this, the longest scene in the play, with three short sequences each of which requires Vasques to present a different persona. In this, the first, we are shocked not just by the speed of his changed attitude but to its considerable violence, ordering Putana to be dragged to the coalhouse and there blinded and further mutilated should she resist. We should note, too, his description of her as an 'old, damnable hag', 'hag' being for Ford's audience synonymous with 'witch', an infernally wicked woman.

**233–8**   But the change from this behaviour to his brief soliloquy is just as arresting, as Vasques expresses moral horror at the depravity of this sexual liaison between brother and sister, while himself equating this with a sexual pun: how a 'smooth tale' (smart story/ penis) can outwit a 'smooth tail' (or woman/vagina), which is again a meaning difficult for the modern actor (and even perhaps for his Jacobean counterpart) to convey.

**239–50**   The arrival of Giovanni confirms Putana's statement to be as true as the changing seasons, and requires another shift in Vasques. Giovanni, we must assume, has no inkling at this point that his sister's pregnancy is known to Soranzo, nor, more important in the playing, that his own role in the affair has been revealed. The sub-text remains sexual: Giovanni's suggestion that his sister's 'new sickness' is caused by her over-indulgence in 'the flesh' (i.e. she's eaten too much meat) is read by Vasques – always keen to find the most crude meaning in any double-entendre – as a reference to 'penis', his focus on her sexual activity prompting the ironic description of her as 'virtuous'. As Giovanni exits, tipping Vasques for his information, Soranzo enters. Or Vasques may need to see Soranzo first, alerting him that Annabella is now alone.

*Although Giovanni is here invited to go up to his sister's room, he has not arrived by V.i when Annabella gives the Friar a note of warning for her brother, which we see delivered in V.iii, and the couple are not seen together until V.v. The logic of this sequence, which requires us to imagine an overlapping time scheme, may trouble some critics but is unlikely to bother an audience.*

**251–end of act**   It is possible that rather than 'I am made a man', Ford had Vasques claim to be 'a made man', meaning totally successful in his activities and a common seventeenth-century expression. But the line as printed can mean the same thing. His reference to his 'cue' sustains the notion of his ever-changing role-playing, each new performance determined by the situation he is presented with. Soranzo's line confirms that none of what has happened will be known to Giovanni, and he may expect a brother to take some action in response. Vasques assures him that Putana, the most likely person to divulge events, has been dealt with. Soranzo is caught between frustration at having to behave gently to Annabella rather than letting loose his revenge (his image compares himself to an animal tied to a stake running round and round, unable to escape) and his fear. What he is afraid of is not entirely clear: presumably either of reprisals against him or it being publicly known that he has married a woman already pregnant by another man. Too distracted, perhaps, he does not seem to pick up on Vasques's indication of Giovanni's complicity. But all will soon be revealed.

# Act V

## Act V, scene i

**0 SD *Enter* ANNABELLA above**    The stage direction repeats that of Annabella's first appearance in 1.ii, except that where she was then accompanied by Putana, this is the first time she has been alone on stage. Some editors add '[with a letter written in blood]' to the stage direction at the opening of the scene. A similar letter is used in *The Spanish Tragedy* by Thomas Kyd, first performed at the Rose playhouse, which though outdoors was, like the Phoenix, small in comparison to playhouses like the Theatre or Globe, and suggests that the audience (or at least some) could see for themselves the red writing.

**1–10**    An Annabella very different from the explosively defiant woman of IV. iii now presents herself. Conventionally, a character in soliloquy speaks the truth as she or he sees it, leaving the audience to take a position in relation to what is said. Now she appears resigned, the passionate pleasures of her relationship with Giovanni seen as pointless moments from a life which she now wants to leave. (Giovanni, it appears, was right to fear that she would be susceptible to pressure on her faith and conscience.) Aware, it seems, that events are moving fast, she welcomes that haste, wishing that Time (seen as often in early modern plays as a 'post', or messenger) should pause in his ride only to gather up her story and tell it to future times as a warning of her own wretched life, that her own 'woeful woman's tragedy' will become (in keeping with the play's overarching metatheatricality) akin to the very play the audience is watching. Indeed, l. 8 seems clearly intended to echo the final couplet of *Romeo and Juliet* ('For never was a story of more woe, / Than this of Juliet and her Romeo'), underlining that, in both plays, misery was ultimately the woman's (spelt 'woeman' in the Folio edition of Shakespeare's play) lot.

**11–24**    At this moment the Friar enters (on the main stage in Ford's playhouse, with Annabella on the balcony above). Her word 'confess' recalls both her own earlier encounter with the Friar in III. vi and (if it is conceived as a post-confession scene) Giovanni's in the opening scene of the play. The Friar's arrival coincides with her explicit acceptance of her guilt, and of the 'vile unhappiness' and barren loneliness, deprived of Giovanni and physical love, to which her lust has brought her. Her words also imagine her conscience as a prosecutor with the 'depositions' against her made by those she has wronged, written in her own guilt and recognizing that external beauty is nothing compared with inner virtue. Interestingly, although she sees Giovanni as having destroyed his own virtues and plundered her own reputation, she sees him also as the victim of some fault in her, of the bad luck that could have been predicted at her birth. And consequently she wishes that any punishment, mortal or spiritual, that follows from their relationship should fall on her, not him; that she should be the one to burn in the hell so graphically described by the Friar in III.vi. Lines 19–20 clearly echo *Dr Faustus*, 'You stars that reigned at my nativity, / Whose influence hath allotted death and hell' (V.ii.154–5), which, as Leech notes, 'can hardly be accidental, and it brings with it the notion of a terrified submission' (1957: 56).

**24–37** The Friar's attention is caught by the penitent confession he hears, and Annabella's line completes his, underlining the fact that she thinks she is not overheard by any on-stage character. Clearly, the encounter in III.vi was not the only time he tried to steer her towards another life but in the event she took no notice, challenged heaven's law against incest, and now reaps the penalty for that, an admission that brings comfort to the Friar. Now she wishes that her guardian angel (see II.ii.154) would send her someone to take the letter confessing her guilt, written in her own blood and stained with her tears. That done, she will repent, and turn away from life – her life of sin with Giovanni; the verb 'die' carried the idea of sexual release, and in which she has already, in effect, died spiritually – and welcome her physical death.

**37–end of scene** Annabella's request for the Friar to identify himself reminds us of her query from the same stage position in I.ii, and is another of the repetitions (of action, gesture, blocking or language) through which Ford traces and underlines the impact of the journey characters make through the play, just as the Friar's reference to her 'free confession' again keeps in our minds the difference between this Annabella and the one we saw in III.vi. Her repentance is so heart-felt that it is written in her own blood, but it reminds us too, of how little she knows of events since she parted from Soranzo to be confined in her chamber, 'Barred of all company', and especially is suspicious of the reason why Putana has not been allowed to see her. More important, she fears not only for Giovanni's soul, encouraging him, too, to repent, but for his life, as she recognizes that Soranzo cannot be trusted, and wants to warn her brother of Vasques's busy activity in rooting out what's going on. Left alone, assured by the Friar that he will convey the letter to Giovanni, she concludes with a couplet, its form embodying the closure not only of this scene, but of her sense of an approaching ending and willing acceptance of her death.

## Act V, scene ii

**1–end of scene**   Vasques is set upon stirring up Soranzo's anger, with a summary of the humiliation Soranzo has suffered, and with the final taunt that a cuckold is too weak to take action against the wrongs done to him. But Soranzo needs no further encouragement. Clearly, the tethered beast of his revenge has been working itself to a frenzy and he is ready to let it off the leash. However, that has not led him to rush blindly in. He has a plan, seeing himself in the role of Othello, wanting Annabella to dress herself again in her bridal gown, when he will (as Vasques urged him earlier) treat her gently and with love – at first, anyway. However, his immediate shift to demand that Vasques's banditti be ready in ambush reveals this is all part of his plan. Vasques still seems concerned that Soranzo should keep his mind on revenge and leave the details to him, but Soranzo has had time to think, and issues his own instructions: there will be another feast to match the one at the wedding (which we know included a murder), but this time Giovanni's double role as his 'brother-rival' (19) is known to him. Again Vasques urges him not to let his pity overcome him (though what the evidence is for this anxiety about Soranzo's innate good nature is not clear from the preceding action). Soranzo, however, appears totally committed to his revenge.

## Act V, scene iii

**1– 16**   Giovanni's soliloquy (which directly mirrors Annabella's in V.i), with its Faustian echoes, brilliantly reveals his arrogant self-certainty mingled with contempt for those who challenge him, and for the audacity of common opinion that tries to force people to think and behave in ways that are countered by their actual experience, treating them as children who have to be punished of they deviate from that path. His evidence is his own experience: his expectation that his sister's marriage would bring an end to their love making has been confounded, and it is as 'sweet and delicious' (stressing the physical nature of the relationship) as it was at the start of their relationship. We listen to his lecture from the perspective of knowing that, while he may not have changed, his sister certainly appears to have done so, while Giovanni reaffirms his belief that while others may dwell on the life to come, he is focused on the present, immediate, human world.

**17–26** The Friar's entrance underlines the parallel between this scene and V.i, the similarity in staging creating an opportunity to reveal the difference in the sibling's states of mind. Where Annabella recognized the hell described by the Friar, Giovanni dismisses it as a superstition. Indeed, he is confident he 'could prove it', the conditional tense perhaps suggesting that now he's so certain of himself that he doesn't care whether the Friar accepts his argument or not, and so can't be bothered to try. The Friar, too, seems resolved that persuasion is not going to work, and presumably hopes that Annabella's letter will have some impact on Giovanni; but he misjudges the response. (I think lines 25–6, which recall his vivid imagery to Annabella in III.vi., are not an aside as some editors suggest, but are a moment of direct warning to Giovanni about what he is about to read.)

**27–31** The contents of the letter, in such contrast to Giovanni's own thoughts, clearly shock him. But his first reaction is to see it as a further trick of the Friar's, casting him as some kind of agent (though 'factor' also has the sense of someone who buys and sells for someone else, perhaps suggesting Giovanni's attitude to what he sees as the Friar's less than honourable motive). In these exchanges we hear a new tone. Giovanni is not, as he did earlier, seeing the Friar's ideas, though in his view wrong, as determining his qualities as a man. Now he sees the Friar and his 'religion masked sorceries' as one and the same thing, which prompts the Friar's retort that Giovanni has become incapable of feeling, his conscience and heart no longer within reach. ('Seared' means both 'dried up', picking up the 'fruitful' images of Giovanni's earlier speech, as well as 'scorched', as in the fires of hell, and a callous conscience. It is what Peter Brook calls a 'vibrating word', one that carries numerous appropriate meanings, some of which, if not all, are available to members of the audience.)

**31–40** Giovanni completes the Friar's line, but unlike previous arguments where this formal device suggested a link between them, or at least an attempt to find one, here it suggests Giovanni has stopped listening to any talk about warnings and wants to cut the Friar off. Counter to the weight he earlier gives to evidence, although he recognizes Annabella's handwriting and acknowledges that the letter is therefore written in her blood, he totally dismisses what she says: he denies they have been found out, accusing her of cowardice, of wanting to betray and renounce their mutual pleasure, of writing nonsense. Indeed, despite having just accepted that the letter is in her hand, but because he cannot allow these really to be his sister's views, he first claims it is a forgery, or, if it is not, that Annabella has been persuaded to set down the spiteful and malignant views of the Friar.

**41–54** We do not get to hear the Friar's response to this charge, as Vasques's entrance interrupts their row, though Giovanni's query to Vasques no doubt carries something of his mood and (as we saw in IV.i) his earlier attitude to these intrusions. Vasques's polite and measured invitation is a strong contrast to the vigorous exchange that precedes it, and the rhythm, though not the mood of the scene alters. Vasques, as we have seen in all his exchanges, is constantly alert to the words people use. Here, he picks up on Giovanni's response that he will 'dare' come to Soranzo's feast (presumably testing whether Giovanni suspects what might be planned), and, when Giovanni asserts that not only does he dare, but that he 'will' come, Vasques presses him further, to state unequivocally that he will be there.

**55–63** The nature of Vasques's probing is enough to alert the Friar that something is up, but not Giovanni, who is clearly so exercised by events that he is not thinking straight. The Friar is right to be certain that this is a plot against Giovanni, but not only has he lost his position of trust with Giovanni, but his use of the word 'ruled' is too provocative: if Giovanni won't be ruled by heaven, or his own conscience, or even his sister's pleading, he certainly won't be ruled by any man, especially one he no longer trusts. His response shows that, like Macbeth, he is also a man who has gone so far that he cannot go back. Moreover, he now is prepared to challenge even Death and all threats that might be made against him. He will go, and will be as violent to them as they wish to be to him.

**63–70**   This shared line will be the last between them, and it seals their final separation with its repeat of 'go'. The Friar, certain of the 'bad, fearful end' that awaits Giovanni, declares himself unable to stay to see this person, to whom he has been devoted, indeed loved, meet such a fate, which will not cease with his death but lead him to the terrors the Friar has articulated so vehemently.

*The Friar's departing line, that he leaves Giovanni to 'despair', is more significant than a modern audience might suppose. 'Despair' is the state of mind in which men and women lose faith in God's power to save them, the state of mind in which someone might take his or her life. It is, for example, the state to which the Duchess of Malfi's brother, Ferdinand, wishes to reduce her through the relentless tortures and miseries he subjects her to in Act IV of that play. Bergetto's death in III.vii pointed the way to the play's tragic conclusion, and the Friar's departure also has a broader thematic implication, as 'the symbol of true religion leaves the city, corruption and hypocrisy go unchallenged, and the powerful cardinal is made a kind of symbol of the society's venality' (Stavig 1968: 120).*

**71–end of scene**   Giovanni's defiant response to the Friar, called to him as he exits, may remind us of Romeo's 'Here, here will I remain / With worms that are thy chambermaids. O here / Will I set up my everlasting rest' (V.iii.108–10), an echo that underlines Ford's portrayal of Giovanni's 'grotesquely exaggerated copy' of the mood and actions of Shakespeare's character (Smallwood 1981: 65). Giovanni is now more alone than at any point in the play. But whereas Annabella has confessed that 'My conscience now stands up against my lust' (V.i.9), and seems to seek some reconciliation with the world around her and its values, Giovanni seeks no such settlement. Defiantly, he summons his strength to break free of conventional behaviour ('old prescription') that might deflect him from his path, even if his need to prove himself stronger than all around him leads to a 'glorious death'. However, as we have already seen with the death of Bergetto, however careful the planning, the power to determine the identity of the shrubs that might be crushed if he, the oak, falls, may not be his to determine.

## Act V, scene iv

**1–18** Soranzo and Vasques brief the banditti about their task. (Banditti had a reputation for their violent assaults on travellers in the mountainous region between Parma and the port of Genoa, the same area where Hippolita believed Richardetto to have been murdered on his unnecessary journey to Livorno.) Soranzo withholds nothing that will spur them on, offering not just gold but pardon for their offences, so allowing these outlaws to return to society. We have seen these men in action against Putana, but their presence here is particularly potent, following on straight after Giovanni's defiance.

**19–33** After the banditti depart, Vasques, having assured Soranzo that the plan proceeds, clearly sees the need again to assure himself that Soranzo is not losing his desire for vengeance. He reminds Soranzo of the wrongs he has suffered beyond just those enacted by Giovanni and Annabella. It might strike us as odd to see 'Hippolita's blood' listed among these revenge-worthy wrongs, given that Vasques murdered her in protecting his master, but as we have seen elsewhere in the play, characters frequently and randomly come up with excuses to justify their bloody behaviour, exposing the double standards that prevail in Parma. Soranzo's response is to remind Vasques that though he may not keep talking about it his desire for revenge burns bright, and that only blood will satisfy him. For Vasques, this is a sign that he is starting to sound like a true Italian, a race renowned in the English popular imagination for not only their obsession with revenge, but their capacity to exercise it in elaborate and often terrifyingly violent ways. Having assured himself of Soranzo's commitment, Vasques is now concerned that he understands that Giovanni (the 'incest-monger' as he calls him, with his characteristic linguistic flair), who will come eager to satisfy his sexual urges with his sister, must be given time and space to fall into their trap. It is clearly Vasques's plan that Giovanni should be killed by the banditti in the very act of intercourse with his sister and so, with no chance to repent this mortal sin (not something we've heard Giovanni be concerned about), go straight to hell.

**34–45**  No sooner has Soranzo agreed, than Giovanni appears. It is a moment that needs to be held on stage as, for the first time, Soranzo confronts the man whose identity he so violently tried to extract from Annabella, while Giovanni knows (however boldly he tried to brush the idea away) that he is facing a man who wants him dead. Both know that Soranzo's courteous welcome is a sham. Soranzo is keen to know that Florio (who he seems determined should witness the exposure of his children's sins) has arrived, Giovanni keen to see his sister. Soranzo is playing his part well, casually courteous, making a small joke as he suggests Giovanni (who he repeatedly addresses as 'brother') should seek her out while he looks after his other guests. But even that joke has a sharp edge to it: a secondary meaning of 'housewife', 'in Soranzo's mouth though not in Giovanni's ears' (Wiggins 2003) is 'hussy' – a trollop or slut

**46–end of scene**  As Giovanni exits, with Vasques perhaps reassuring Soranzo – who might be finding it difficult to keep cool – that Giovanni is going to his death, the arrival is announced of the Cardinal. The trio on stage make an interesting image as they stand complimenting each other in pre-dinner small talk: two would-be murderers and a corrupt churchman.

## Act V, scene v

**0**In Ford's playhouse, the bed would probably have been pushed out with the two actors already on it (White 2009).

**1–29**  The scene obviously parallels the opening of II.i, though now we have not only moved inside the bed-chamber but to the bed itself, the site of their incestuous union. The tone could not be more different, however. Gone is Giovanni's near-playful insistence that Annabella must have a husband. Her mood is as it was at the end of V.i, and his sexual jealousy is at full-pitch as he misreads her reluctance to continue their sexual relationship. She tries to get him to see sense, or at least recognise the danger he is in, which prompts from him the most complete statement to date of his belief that everything depended on their mutual commitment, that he could guide their fate had she just remained faithful. In other words, he sees the failure as hers, her weakness and infidelity in not staying true to their love. Again, patiently and lovingly, she tries to get him to see the reality of their situation: that the extravagant feast, the instruction by Soranzo (V.ii.9–10) that she should dress in her bridal gown (her 'gay attires'), the decision to release her from her solitary confinement, are all part of a deliberate plan, and that the banquet (and she may recognize its ironic parody of her wedding) is the precursor (harbinger) to the scene of their deaths. In some early, uncorrected copies of the play, her phrase is 'dying time'. All modern editions alter this to 'dining time' (which would have been printed 'dyning time', and explains the error, if that's what it is), but the uncorrected words may carry a resonance truer to the moment.

**29–37**　Giovanni jumps in to rebut her argument. Florio commented in I.iii that Giovanni was 'devoted to his book', and unlike Soranzo's predilection for love poetry, Giovanni has clearly been reading St Thomas Aquinas. He points out that the view expressed in the Book of Revelation, that 'the first heaven and the first earth were passed away; and there was no more sea', was an idea which scholastic philosophers such as St Thomas Aquinas (known, disparagingly, as 'schoolmen' – we may recall the Friar's rebuke to Giovanni in I.i), had attempted to rationalize. However, Giovanni focuses on the hole in that argument that had troubled St Augustine (*City of God* 20, 16): that whereas the Stoics had taught that the seas would gradually dry up in the heat, the idea of a destruction that is instantaneous and complete ('all this globe… consumed to ashes in a minute') requires one to believe that water will burn. In other words, Giovanni is saying that if he is to believe that their love can come to an end so abruptly, then he must, too, believe that water can burn, and if that were so – and this is the real core of the speech in what it tells us of his state of mind – only then would he believe also in the existence of heaven and hell. He brushes aside Annabella's assertion of the certainty that both do exist as no more than a dream, since if there were an afterlife he and his sister would meet in it which, with the same lack of hesitancy with which she confessed her love for him, she confirms by completing his line.

**38–66**　In a manner reminiscent of the eagerness with which he clung to a life-line thrown by the Friar in I.i (l. 68) his tone and attitude seem to change on an instant, as he seeks reassurance from her that they will, after death, indeed enjoy exactly the same pleasures as on earth. She, more sanguine, as she has been since the beginning of this act, diverts him from thoughts of a future to the dangers they face now. Their next exchange identifies the difference in how they view themselves and their situation: to her, he is a troubled and distracted young man, while he sees himself as the embodiment of Death, angered and seeking revenge. She sees her brother crying, he sees himself shedding tears on her grave, tears such as he wept when he thought he loved her in vain, tears which are a tribute to his love for her and hers for him. His speech develops into, essentially, a requiem, a eulogy that might be spoken over her grave, as he acknowledges they must part, she to find a place among the saints in heaven, he to carry out his 'swift repining wrath'. His words to her might seem curious from a man who has so vehemently denied conventional notions of heaven and hell. Michael Neill describes Giovanni's behaviour as an attempt 'to dress the murder in the sainted trappings of a martyrdom' (1988: 161, while Janet Clare suggests that here 'Ford is sacrificing psychological credibility for high emotion' (2006, 112), but the moment might equally remind us of Giovanni at the start of the play, desperate to find some comfort, even a solution to his desire, in faith.

**67–78**    What Annabella understands from his lines is not entirely clear, though it is possible that she acknowledges the need for a suicide pact. His funeral elegy, his references to her death and ascent to heaven clearly signal her imminent death, as she looks to the angels for protection. But protection from whom? He speaks gently and lovingly of their relationship as something in the past, but is sure that when society understands how strong their love was for each other, despite the unacceptable nature of the relationship, and although, as Giovanni accepts, their condemnation will be just, they will forgive this incest as they would not others (an attitude that lies at the core of much critical discussion of the play). He takes her hand, chiding Nature for the healthiness of Annabella at the moment she approaches death. Again they kiss, and she willingly gives him the forgiveness he asks for: Annabella may have renounced their sexual relationship, but clearly not the love she feels for him and her care for his safety.

**79–94** She is clearly surprised at his sudden farewell (and given Ford's care to impress his departure on us in II.i.31–4, we might recall it now). But Giovanni's answer is not immediately clear – for once the second half of the line is not a response to the first – as he begins an invocation to the sun to darken its rays so that the world may not behold the deed, a near-blasphemous moment as he seeks a response equal to that at the moment of Christ's death on the cross. She clearly senses that something is wrong, that his 'Farewell' marks her departure, not his. And with one more request for a kiss (there are close parallels throughout the scene with the final acts of *Othello* and *Romeo and Juliet*), he stabs her, the act embracing the twin poles of sex and death which have marked the extremes of their relationship, and (for Giovanni) an act of honourable revenge that supersedes the duties of love. But revenge on who? Annabella for marrying? Soranzo for taking her away? The world for refusing to bend to his desire? And having observed him and Soranzo over the past two acts, their vaunting claims that revenge is brave and honourable will appear hollow and self-serving. Interestingly, in response to her question why he should kill her, he refuses to answer, at least until she is dead, as to do so might cause him to hesitate (stagger) and divert him from what he sees as a glorious deed. As Annabella dies, the victim of Giovanni's appalling and inhuman act, she begs forgiveness from Heaven for Giovanni, but does not, it should be noted, forgive him herself. As she has throughout the play she again underlines their sibling relationship, but now uses that against him, *unkind* carrying the meaning both of 'cruel' and 'unnaturally wicked', a betrayal of the love and protection expected of one of her own kin, or family. Havelock Ellis, a great admirer of Ford and his work, nevertheless considered this 'feeble exclamation' fell short of the 'tragic height of passion' in a moment of rare 'failure of insight' on the playwright's part, but I think most audiences would more likely agree that 'there is as much resonance and more meaning in the pathos of Annabella's dying words… than there is in Giovanni's triumphant but disjunctive revenge rhetoric' (Clare 2006: 112).

**95–end of scene** As Giovanni underlines that he knows he has not only murdered his sister, but also their son, it becomes clear that his revenge has been to prevent Soranzo possessing her, a terrible, perverted conclusion to his increasingly demented possessiveness.

Looking at her body, lamenting her death while seeing it as a triumph over a scandalous reputation, or the hate of those around them, he urges himself on to some even more demanding task before he can complete his part in a revenge play-within-a-play of which he is both author and leading actor. But, of course, Annabella is not, as Giovanni sees her – and wants us to see her too – as 'over-glorious' in her wounds, 'triumphing over infamy and hate' (104–5). She is dead.

## Act V, scene vi

**0  A** *banquet.* **Enter CARDINAL, FLORIO, DONADO, SORANZO, RICHARDETTO, VASQUES** *and* **Attendants;** *they take their places.*   The third banquet of the play, and the second we have seen on stage. The first banquet (I.ii, offstage) broke up in a quarrel that spilled on to the street and might easily have ended in a death, and after the events of IV. i, even an audience not *au fait* with a banquet's general significance in early modern plays will be alert to the mayhem that is likely to follow now. At this point however nothing should be signalling that: of those on stage, only Soranzo and Vasques know exactly what has happened to alter the situation since these characters were all together earlier at Soranzo and Annabella's wedding.

**1–9**   Vasques is still encouraging Soranzo to be resolute, but his master appears calm and resolved, turning smoothly to the Cardinal with a simple piece of polite small talk before casually enquiring where Giovanni is.

**10–21**   The tone of normality is crucial, as it allows the play to settle following Giovanni's exit with his sister's body at the end of V.v and his entrance here, now with a heart stuck on the blade of his dagger. With all the other characters seated, Ford has prepared a stage within a stage for Giovanni, and an image that recalls or prefigures the revenger, Orgilus, in *The Broken Heart*, standing with his wrists slit, as his blood pours from him, his arm bound 'that so the pipes may from their conduits / Convey a full stream' (V.ii.102–3). The image of Giovanni with the heart, and the structure of its metaphoric associations that has recurred throughout the play in deeds and language has now become a grim and terrifying reality. Unlike Orgilus, Giovanni is now beyond

our sympathy and even understanding. The vision he presents is carefully described: 'trimmed' literally means decorated (just as we use it of
a Christmas tree), but with the added sense of being dressed up for a
special occasion, here by being covered in the steaming, fresh blood of
Annabella and, by implication, that of the unborn child in her womb.
The striking juxtapositions of 'love' and 'vengeance' (12) and, later, of
'glorious' and 'executioner' (33) reveal how distorted his reasoning has
become. Responses to him from those on stage are mixed: wonder,
amazement and, in Soranzo's case (perhaps in an aside to Vasques
or the audience, and repeating his characteristic self-regard), concern
that Giovanni has outwitted him and seized the initiative. As Giovanni
elaborates on 'the rape of life and beauty / Which I have acted', his reference to his sister strikes a note of alarm in Florio.

**21–54**   The next sequence of the scene is extraordinary, even by the
high standards of Jacobean plays to shock an audience. Giovanni's
appearance echoes the icons of Revenge common in Jacobean
emblems, enforced by the sheer, chilling brilliance of the language,
with its images of cannibalism and anatomy. The heart 'digged' (the
verb perfectly catching the obscene violence of his act) from her
body, being, for him, the prize of his act of love and vengeance, an
act that not even Fate, even less ordinary mortals, could prevent him
from carrying out. Surrounded by the physical image of the banquet,
Giovanni uses it to characterize his own 'feast', and as we have seen
throughout the play, Ford sets the character's language and actions
at odds with each other, not merely ironically, as with, for example,
the classical references during their love-making, but now with the
power of the radical disconnections of the Grotesque, embodying
the dizzying confusion of the fictional audience to Giovanni's
performance, and the responses of the 'real' audience in the theatre.
As if offering a scientific specimen of particular interest, he shows
the heart to them, moving from character to character, letting them
take a closer look, asking if they can put a name to its owner. Their
responses, all asking what he means, is he mad, and so on, derive
from a refusal, or incapacity, to confront what must be growing in
their minds as an explanation. Displaying the heart, he identifies it as
his sister's, and explains to his father the nature of his and Annabella's
bond, and how it was only the pregnancy that revealed their relationship. His dislike of his father – presumably, if irrationally, for

encouraging the match with Soranzo – may be what drives the brutality of his language to him. (Ford's use of ' happy passage' at l. 49 – which implies both a sequence of events and an exchange of amorous experience between lovers – may have been prompted by Shakespeare's 'fearful passage of their death-marked love', *Romeo and Juliet*, Prologue, 9.) 'Paler cheek' (46) means either paler than his own blood-stained face, or paler than Florio's, whose responses seem a mix of genuine revulsion and shock, but also come from an awareness that these family catastrophes are being aired not only in public, but in front of the Cardinal, as sharing l. 51 makes clear ('rage' means 'frenzy', or 'madness' rather than 'anger'). But those present still doubt (or are unable to conceive) that this heart really is Annabella's and Vasques is sent to bring her to them.

**55–9**   To bridge the time it takes for Vasques to return, Giovanni again emphasizes the truth of what he says, his description of his feelings for her – 'by the love / I bore my Annabella while she lived' – set against the uncompromising description of his acts against her body: 'These hands have from her bosom ripped this heart'. It is the blazon made flesh.

   *In the space of a few lines (V.v.24–5; 31–2; 59), Giovanni draws again and again on the image of 'ripping' to explain to the dumbfounded guests exactly what he has done to his sister. In the heat of the moment of performance, however, we are unlikely to have time to reflect upon what has been a pattern of usage throughout the play. Right at the start of their relationship Giovanni invited his sister to do to him precisely what he ultimately does to her, when he offered his dagger so that she could 'Rip up my bosom' to 'behold his heart' (I.ii.204–6) and discover the truth of his intentions (see p. 0 for discussion of the metaphorical significance of a heart). In III.vi, the Friar predicts that Annabella's brother's kisses will kisses will seem like 'daggers' points', and refers to the 'new motions' of her 'heart'. IV.iii.53–4, Soranzo threatened to 'rip up' Annabella's bosom in his furious efforts to learn the name of the father of Annabella's child, and a slightly different form of the same act of discovery is expressed by the Friar when he delivers Annabella's warning letter, written in her own blood, to Giovanni with the invitation to him to 'Unrip the seal and see' (V.iii.24) the danger they are in. The metaphor of flesh-ripping is found elsewhere in Ford's plays when characters – especially in extremis – seek to reveal their own or another's inmost thoughts or secrets (Love's Sacrifice, The Broken Heart, Perkin Warbeck).*

**60–8 *Enter* VASQUES**    The stage direction in Q1633 does not indicate whether Vasques comes simply reporting what he has seen, or actually carrying Annabella's mutilated the body. In production, however, the latter is frequently the case, as it more effectively prompts Florio's collapse (his, too, is a 'broken heart') than a mere verbal confirmation might seem to. The Cardinal's line, too, may be clarified by the actions that accompany it. Either the Cardinal does not register that Florio has died, and is encouraging him to be resolute in the face of events, or (an interpretation supported by l. 62), is instructing the Attendants to show Giovanni the body of his father, an image that mirrors Giovanni displaying the heart of his sister. Giovanni's response to his father's demise, however, reveals that to him it is no more than a neat addition to the pattern of familial deaths.

**69–71**    Challenged by Soranzo, Giovanni, who began the play believing the fates 'have doomed my death' (I.ii.140) shows how far he has moved, repeating the claim he made earlier (III.ii.20), that the Fates who spin, weave and cut the thread of human life are now in his control. In this moment, most clearly, he sees himself as the justifiable agent of death, whether his sister's or father's, so absolving himself from guilt for his actions. However, his reference to being 'gilt', or smeared in, their blood (l. 67) will sound to the audience like 'guilt'.

**72–4**    In order to stab Soranzo, although it would be possible to push on through the heart so that the blade enters Soranzo's body, it is possible that Giovanni has by now removed it from his dagger (perhaps on 'this heart', l. 72). The combination of dagger, heart and stabbing is open to a number of actions: Kenneth Cranham (in the 1980 TV version placed the heart, wrapped in paper, on the table before Soranzo, like a butcher serving a customer; Jonathan Cullen (RSC, 1991–2) gave the heart to Soranzo ('thus I exchange it royally for thine'); and in Griffi's 1971 film Giovanni took Soranzo's own weapon from him and tried to kill him.

**75–87**    With Soranzo wounded and incapacitated, Vasques launches himself on Giovanni. As he did with Grimaldi in II.ii, it seems that this practised killer soon has the better of Giovanni, but despite repeated stabbings he refuses to die. Vasques calls (using the signal 'Vengeance!', agreed in V.iv.13–14) for the banditti to finish him off (though apart from creating an image of Giovanni, like a trapped animal and surrounded by killers) it is not immediately clear to me why Vasques (not a coward from what we have seen of him) requires their intervention.

**88–100**   Vasques's first thought is for Soranzo who is close to death, but Soranzo finds comfort in that Giovanni's imminent death means his honour has been revenged (though his last instruction to his servant is to ensure that Giovanni *does* die), and the fact that Giovanni is still in fact alive may well prompt an audience's derisive laughter. Vasques's words to the dead Soranzo suggest the affection and loyalty he feels towards his master (an echo perhaps of Poggio at the death of Bergetto). More surprisingly, is the way this tone seems to be carried into his exchange with Giovanni, almost gently explaining how he gave Giovanni his first wound before Giovanni's impudence brings that to a close. Farr states (1979: 53) that Vasques's phrase 'I was your first man sir' (95) was what Thames boatmen used to claim a customer, which would suggest that he has, indeed, become Giovanni's Charon, his ferryman to death.

**101–7**   Now the Cardinal steps in, encouraging Giovanni to seek repentance before death. But Giovanni underlines that, given the death of Annabella, the death wounds he has received are the only mercy he requires, and that Death is a late, but most welcome, guest at this banquet. As he dies, perhaps recalling his last conversation with his sister, he remains steadfast in his hope of finding 'grace', but to him that will be the chance 'freely to view' her face and to spend time still with her, though even in death, he sees her as his possession.

**108–31**   With the main protagonists dead, the remaining plot ends need to be tied up. Although he reassures the Cardinal that these events are not part of some larger revolt, Vasques is still, in the Cardinal's eyes, the enemy of Grimaldi (hence a 'wretched villain, incarnate fiend'). In response, Vasques explains first that he is Spanish by birth, and that his loyalty to Soranzo sprang from a duty to Soranzo's father whom he had served and loved, a service he extended to Soranzo. As has been the case throughout this scene, and indeed, the play as a whole, this moment of quiet reflection by Vasques is followed by the information – made more disturbing by the matter-of-fact manner in which it is delivered – that Putana, her eyes put out on his orders as punishment for turning a blind eye to the siblings' betrayal of Soranzo, is alive and locked in 'this' (i.e. an adjacent) room, where, presumably, she has been able to hear everything that has gone on.

**132–46** The Cardinal now begins to dispense his 'justice'. It is not immediately clear whether it is Putana or Annabella who is to be burnt as an 'example' to others. The description of her as 'chief in these effects' would suggest Annabella, as would the agreement of Donado (the closest she has to a family member now) to oversee it. However, 'sentence' clearly means to condemn someone to a punishment, and it is unusual to talk of sentencing someone already dead, which might mean that it is Putana (though she is hardly 'chief' in the whole business) who faces the stake as the main criminal, when we know that she was at most an accomplice. She has already suffered blinding (a punishment echoing Oedipus's penalty for witnessing the incest with his mother) and now must be burnt, as the Cardinal reveals the violent underbelly of the church. In the last confession in the play, Vasques reveals the depth of his loyalty to Soranzo and stoically accepts that he, too, may face death, leaving it to the Cardinal's 'reason' to judge his fate. The Cardinal – 'that protector of well-born criminals' (Roper 1975: lv) – duly commutes a death sentence to banishment on 'grounds of reason, not of thine offence'. As Hogan shrewdly notes, the Cardinal and Vasques are 'brothers under the skin... both of them focus with Old Testament rigor on the heinousness of sexual aberration, symbolized by Vasques' blinding of the suggestively named old nurse Putana, and the Cardinal's burning of her' (1977: 315). Vasques's exit line would surely have encouraged some response from the original audience used to seeing plays about revenge set generally in Italy, and Jonathan Hyde got a big laugh too in the 1991 RSC production. It isn't clear whether Vasques has a particular Italian in mind, or whether it is just a claim to general superiority in revenge. He might mean Giovanni, or possibly Soranzo (who had begun to 'turn Italian' (V.iv.28), which may suggest the 'previously devoted servant is showing a new independence of mind now that his obligations to the Soranzo family are done' (Wiggins 2003).

**147–56**  Florio, Soranzo and Giovanni have all died without anyone to inherit their wealth. Nevertheless, the Cardinal's use of 'confiscate' and 'seized upon' reveal the sharp practice he now engages in, and one completely in line with the shifty and self-interested morality he displayed in III.ix. Nicholas Brooke (1979: 109) suggests that the Cardinal is not represented as 'so hopelessly corrupt' as Webster's are, but it is hard to locate the positive side of this character. There may be a danger that the revelation of Richardetto's true identity at this point is close to bathos, producing laughter when a production may not be seeking it. No one, certainly, will be thinking about him. On the other hand, all through the play, and as he repeats now, Richardetto has interpreted the acts around him and their punishment as the 'effect of pride and lust', but this may prompt us to reject this as too trite a response to the complex relationships we have tracked through the play, especially from a man whose aim throughout has been revenge on his wife and Soranzo, and who has hidden himself in a disguise.

**156–end of play**  In fact, this revelation is in a sense another form of the 'neat' ending provided by the Cardinal's final words. Nevertheless, the Cardinal's metadramatic observation that 'never yet / Incest and murder have so strangely met' remains a true statement of our experience of the play, and of its place in Jacobean drama. Lisa Hopkins has argued that the closing line, which (as Ford does in other plays) includes the play's title, has 'strikingly little reference to the audience's fundamental experiences' of the play. I am wary of claiming to know what response, or even which audience, we can assess with confidence, but the fact that the words are printed in italics may indicate that Ford wants to emphasize them, and we may also at this moment recall Donado's cry when the Cardinal took Grimaldi into his protection: 'Is this a churchman's voice? Dwells justice here? (III. ix.62). There is no suggestion that things will change in Parma, where corruption still remains the order of the day, and the trite rhyme of the Cardinal's smug assessment is surely designed to draw attention to its deficiency as a reaction to what we have seen, underlined by the repetition of the play's title which forces us to assess our own response. There has surely been enough for us, indeed, to 'pity'

Annabella, while not losing sight of her decision to embark on an illicit sexual relationship nor her attempt to cover up the results by marrying someone else. If I am correct, this multifaceted response seems to me to be appropriate for a play that has throughout sought to keep us in a state of suspended judgement, held between compassion and condemnation, warning us not to be absolute in our judgements, and our judgement of Annabella above all.

# 3   *Intellectual and Cultural Context*

## Sources

Originality seems to have mattered to John Ford. In the prologue to what is very likely his first independent play, *The Lover's Melancholy* (1628), Ford declared that 'in the following scenes he doth not owe / To others' fancies, nor hath lain in wait / For any stol'n invention', and 20 years later, in the prologue to *The Fancies, Chaste and Noble*, published towards the end of his career, he still thought it necessary to refer to 'his free invention'. However, although he does not claim as much for *'Tis Pity*, and while no particular source for the play has been identified, Ford was clearly influenced not only by a number of works of poetry (including by John Donne, whose lines are often directly echoed in the play) and prose, but also by the plays of dramatists who preceded or worked alongside him. Moreover, *'Tis Pity* closely resembles other of his own plays in putting his characters in complex, seemingly intractable, personal relationships, and making the obstacles they face in negotiating those even more complicated by the particular social or family setting in which the action unfolds. Indeed, when Richard Crashaw wrote 'Thou cheat'st us, Ford: mak'st one seem two by art: / What is *Love's Sacrifice* but *The Broken Heart*', he could as well have added *'Tis Pity* to his list. And Julie Sanders could be referring to Ford when she writes:

> Texts feed off each other and create other texts, and other critical studies; literature creates other literature. Part of the sheer pleasure of the reading experience must be the tension between the familiar and the new, and the recognition both of similarity and difference, between ourselves and between texts. The pleasure exists, and persists, then, in the act of reading in, around, and on (and on). (2006: 14)

The prose sources Ford may have turned to cannot be identified for certain. Claims have been made for a diverse range, including a French story by François de Rosset, 'Des Amours Incestueuses d'un Frère et d'une Soeur', included in *Les Histoires Tragiques de Notre Temps* (Paris, 1615), and there are enough similarities with the play to support Roper's measured view that Ford 'had this story in mind, though perhaps only at the back of his mind' (1975: xxvii). Rosset's sister and brother are the children of a country gentlemen, alike in good looks, and have been apart during the brother's absence at school where he has shone at his studies; the sister is made by her father to marry an older, wealthy man, who, when he learns from a servant of her relationship with her brother, is violent to her before promising forgiveness if she will repent; the discovery of the incest nearly kills their mother with shock, and sister and brother flee to Paris, where she becomes pregnant; and finally, they are discovered and condemned to death, impressing the crowd at their execution with their remorse.

Martin Wiggins (2003) notes that George Whetstone's *Heptameron of Civil Discourses* (1582) includes characters called Bargetto and Soranso, and also proposes *First Fruits, which yield Familiar Speech, Merry Proverbs, Witty Sentences, and Golden Sayings*, primarily a text-book for teaching Italian produced by John Florio and published in 1578; Annabella's sung lines in IV.iii are from the section devoted to 'amorous talk'. (Interestingly, Ford uses the ambiguous phrase 'First Fruits' in the dedicatory letter that precedes the printed text; see p. 4.)

Ford also drew on his own dramatic and non-dramatic work. The Friar's ominous description of hell in III.vi is clearly based on verses from Ford's poem *Christ's Bloody Sweat* (see p. 2):

Here shall the wantons for a downy bed,
Be racked on pallets of still-burning steel.
Here shall the glutton, that hath daily fed
On choice of dainty diet, hourly feel
    Worse meat than toads, and beyond time be drenched
    In flames of fire, that never shall be quenched

Each moment shall the killer be tormented
With stabs that shall not so procure his death;
The drunkard that would never be contented
With drinking up whole flagons at a breath,
    Shall be denied (as he with thirst is stung)
    A drop of water for to cool his tongue.

The influence of the work of other dramatists is obvious, in particular, if to different degrees and in different ways, plays by Kyd, Marlowe, Chapman, Webster, Middleton, Massinger and Shakespeare. The extent of Ford's borrowings led one critic to describe his plays as 'ponderous machines, built from other men's parts' (Frost 1968: 131), but Ford clearly recognized the pointlessness of mere passive repetition, and brought to his own plays new perspectives on moral, intellectual and religious conflicts, viewing them through a prism that was entirely his own. Roland Wymer provides an excellent summary of the position of a writer like Ford, who comes at the end of a particularly productive period of writing:

> All writers of tragedy must engage with and surpass their predecessors in order to achieve the desired emotional effects. Ford's case is special only in that he had more to surpass than most dramatists since his predecessors continued to hold the stage as if they were his most immediate contemporaries rather than revered but distant classics. (1995: 93)

As the leading actor Joseph Taylor observed in the complimentary verse he contributed to Massinger's *The Roman Actor* (1626), in which he had played a leading role and itself a play that draws on others' work, 'No one in these times can produce a play / Worthy his reading, since of late, 'tis true / The old accepted are more than the new' and Ford turned to old plays for inspiration. The opening scene of Act III of George Chapman's *Bussy D'Ambois* (c. 1604) may have provided ideas for *'Tis Pity* II.i, and almost certainly the furious exchanges between Annabella and Soranzo (IV.iii) were shaped by the scene between Tamyra and Montsurry (V.i), while Middleton's *Women Beware Women* (c.1621), as well as portraying an incestuous relationship, may have provided the idea for the Bergetto sub-plot. Ford also drew on earlier plays for smaller, telling details: for example, the potent stage property of a letter written in red ink/blood (V.i) possibly derives from Thomas Kyd's perennially popular revenge play *The Spanish Tragedy* (c. 1588), but Ford weaves it into the thread of variations on 'blood' explored in his play. Similarly, *Antonio and Mellida* (1600), by John Marston, and Shakespeare's *Troilus and Cressida* (c. 1603) may have provided models for the striking image of Annabella and Putana observing Giovanni from the balcony (I.ii), which Ford developed into the defining moment of 'the "uncanny" disclosure of hidden desire in Annabella's recognition of her sexual attraction to her brother' (Wiseman 1990: 188).

Two of Shakespeare's plays, *Othello* and *Romeo and Juliet*, were particularly influential on 'Tis Pity, and other Shakespearean allusions have been suggested by Lisa Hopkins (2002: 101–4; 2010: 3–4). *Othello* was perhaps Shakespeare's best-known play when 'Tis Pity was first performed, a particular favourite of Ford's, and clearly the stimulus for his climactic scene between Giovanni and Annabella where he, like Othello (V.ii.368–9), kills his sister 'in a kiss' (V.v.84). Indeed, *Othello* was such an influence on Ford's later play *Love's Sacrifice* that it 'can too easily seem like a mere hodgepodge of words and stage images from Shakespeare's play' (Moore, 2002: 26). However, Moore's counter-argument that *Love's Sacrifice* in fact 'responds to *Othello* with its own creative devices' (p. 26) offers a perfect description of Ford's much more extensive use in 'Tis Pity of *Romeo and Juliet*. Joan Sargeaunt thought the resemblance between the two plays was limited to 'a superficial likeness' in some character groupings (1966: 124), and Cyrus Hoy asserted baldly that any parallels between these two plays 'are confined to similarities of relatively subordinate character types and that, insofar as the real subjects of the play are concerned, they have next to nothing in common' (1960: 145; he sees Marlowe's *Dr Faustus* as a firmer model). Most critics, however, share Robert Smallwood's view that *Romeo and Juliet* was 'Ford's principal source of inspiration for the general conception and setting of his drama, and for many aspects of its plot, characterization, thematic concerns and conclusion' (1981: 49). Indeed, key moments in 'Tis Pity clearly anticipate that at least some in Ford's audience will have recognised its relationship to *Romeo and Juliet*, and so read it through the 'tension between the familiar and the new' (Sanders, 2006: 14; I have noted these in the Commentary). Fortunately, this productive tension still operates today, given the pervasive popularity of *Romeo and Juliet* on school and university curricula, on stage and through films such as Baz Luhrman's *Romeo + Juliet* and *Shakespeare in Love*. Of course, Ford gave Shakespeare's story a twist by making the lovers in his play brother and sister, the shift from a forbidden to a taboo relationship leading perhaps inevitably to the charges levelled against Ford of 'decadence', of pandering to the increasingly jaded artistic palates of an audience sated with the diet of Jacobean plays by feeding them increasingly sensational themes and scenes.

In fact, the simplest, unanswerable response to those who accuse him of repeating others' voices, is that he succeeded in speaking with a *new* voice of love, grief, hatred, jealousy and all the other human emotions dramatized by his predecessors. And nowhere is this evident than in his use of the controversial theme of incest, and his success in producing a play which, in James Bulman's words, 'challenges conventional morality where others, like [James] Shirley [in *The Traitor*], pandered to it' (1990: 363).

## Incest

The ruling class in different societies at different times have practised incest as a means of keeping power and wealth within the family, including ancient Egypt (the real-life Cleopatra of Shakespeare's play married her brother), early Hawaian and Incan states, as well as, more relevantly to *'Tis Pity*, the Borgias and the Habsburgs, who had encouraged incestuous marriages, especially between uncles and nieces, as a means of consolidating and maintaining land and power within the family (Hopkins, 2002), and within whose power stood the city of Parma. Beyond such aristocratic families, however, incest has been prohibited in virtually all societies by explicit laws supported by popular opinion, with any violation being seen as a sign of both social and sexual depravity. George Sensabaugh asserted that *'Tis Pity She's a Whore* makes a problem of incest' (1944: 153) but there was precious little making to do: within early seventeenth-century English society incest *was* a problem in the sense that it was viewed as a taboo, and that is surely the response that Ford would have anticipated from the majority of his audience. That does not mean, of course, that writers veered away from it, as examples below from classical, medieval and early modern literature will make clear, while the seventeenth century's particular and growing 'fascination with the darker aspects of human psychology' (McCabe 1993: 242) drew playwrights including Tourneur (*The Atheist's Tragedy*), Webster (*The Duchess of Malfi*), Middleton (*Women Beware Women*), Shakespeare (*Pericles*) and Massinger (*The Unnatural Combat*) towards portrayals of aberrant mentalities, including incestuous desire. In Webster's *The Duchess of Malfi*, Ferdinand's desire for his sister borders on the incestuous, though his feelings are in no way returned by the Duchess.

The play was published in 1623 with a commendatory verse by Ford praising it as 'a masterpiece', and it is hardly surprising that Ford found the subject matter so compelling, given that incest is 'the ultimate theme of one who feels the imaginative pull of the frowned-on or forbidden, and yet coercive, passion' (Heilman 1986: 37). Prior to 'Tis Pity, Francis Beaumont and John Fletcher's A King and No King (1611) was undoubtedly the most well-known portrayal of incest between brother and sister, and much of the play seems to prefigure Ford's in its sexual energy. King Arbaces falls passionately in love with his sister, Panthea, and, driven by his uncontrollable but unfulfilled desire, contemplates raping her, or issuing a decree denying she is his sister and so freeing him from any constraints. But at the last minute, when the pressure of passion has reached near bursting point, the play shies away from imminent catastrophe by deft (and credulity stretching) plotting characteristic of its tragi-comic genre, to reveal that the two are not siblings after all, and can legitimately and happily marry. But Ford ducks none of the issues, and it was the uncompromising manner with which he portrayed the incestuous relationship that set him apart from his contemporaries. For example, in Philip Massinger's disturbing play about father–daughter incest, The Unnatural Combat (c. 1624), Malefort Senior's sensual musings about his daughter, Theocrine, sound very like Giovanni's: compare 'I thought it no offence to kiss her often, / Or twine my arms about her softer neck' (IV.i.22–3) with 'Tis Pity, II.i.16–17, for example. But unlike Giovanni, Malefort never loses sight of the true nature of his lust or the collision in him between conscious and unconscious desire – 'Waking, I ne'er cherished obscene hopes, / But in my troubled slumbers often thought / She was too near to me, and then, sleeping, blushed' (IV.i.35–7). Ford, however, and unblushingly, explores what happens when desire becomes action.

## Classical incest

Ovid's story in Book 9 in his Heroides of the incestuous relationship between Canace and her brother, Macareus, a union which produces a child, was perhaps the most influential literary source on writers of Ford's time, probably in the popular translation by George Turbervile (1576 and regularly reprinted). The Book takes the form of letters between lovers. Here, Canace writes to her brother to warn him of

the danger they are in now their relationship is known to their father,
Aeolus.

An Aeolid, who has no health herself, sends it to an Aeolid,
and, armed, these words are written by her hand.
If the script is full of errors, with its dark blots,
the letter will have been stained by a woman's blood.
My right hand holds a pen, my left a naked sword
and the paper's lying loosely in my lap.
This is the image of Aeolus's daughter writing to her brother:
it seems in this way I can appease our harsh father.
I could only wish that he were here to see my death
and the eyes of its author contemplate the act,
though he's uncivilized, and more ferocious than his east wind,
he would gaze at my wounds with dry cheeks.
How can anything good come of living with savage winds…
What's the use of my bandying my ancestor's names about the sky,
that Jupiter can be mentioned among my relatives?
Is this blade, my funeral gift, any less dangerous
because I hold it, not yarn, in my woman's hand?
O I wish, Macareus, the hour that made us one
had come later than the hour of my death!
Brother, why did you love me more than a brother should,
and why was I not merely what a sister should be, to you?
I also burnt with it, in a way I used to hear about,
I don't know what god I felt in my loving heart.
The colour fled from my face, my slender body grew thin,
I took the least food, forced it into my mouth:
I couldn't sleep easily, and the night was a year to me,
and, wounded by no pains, I gave out groans.
Nor could I give a reason for why I acted so,
nor knew what a lover was, but I was one.
My nurse was the first to sense it, with an old woman's acuteness:
my nurse first said: 'Canace, you're in love!'
I blushed, and shame sent my eyes down to my lap:
that was enough of a confession, that silent signal.
Then the burden swelled in my sinful belly,
and the secret load weighed on my weak limbs…
My diligent nurse hides the child among fruits,
and grey olive branches, and light sacred ribbons,
and pretends she's making a sacrifice, says words of prayer:
the people give worship, the father himself steps aside.

Now she was nearly at the door. A cry reached our father's ears
and that betrayed signs of the child…
Aeolus snatched up my baby and revealed the false sacrifice.
The palace echoed to his furious voice.
As the sea trembles, when touched by a mild breeze,
as the ash twig shakes in a warm south wind,
so you might have seen my pale limbs quiver:
the bed was shaken by the body lying on it.
He forced his way in, and broadcast my shame by his shouts,
and scarcely kept his hands from my poor face.
I could do nothing but modestly pour out tears.
My tongue was frozen, numbed by icy fear.
And then he ordered that his little grand-child should be given
to the dogs and birds, abandoned in a lonely place…
He left my room, then at last I beat my breasts
and proceeded to run my fingers through my hair.
Meanwhile one of father's attendants came, with a mournful face,
and his mouth uttered shameful words:
'Aeolus sends you this sword' – he delivered the sword –
'and orders you to know his wish from its purpose.'
I know, and will use the violent weapon bravely:
I will sheath father's gift in my breast.
Do you give me this gift for my marriage, father?
Father, will your daughter be rich in this dowry?
Hymen, betrayed, take your marriage torches far from here,
and flee this impious house with troubled feet!
Furies bear the black torches you bear, to me,
and from those fires light my funeral pyre!…
I too, wounded, will follow the shade of my child:
I will not be called 'mother' or 'bereaved' for long.
Yet you, vain hope of your unhappy sister,
gather I beg you the scattered limbs of your son,
and bring them to their mother, place us in a shared tomb,
and let the narrow urn have whatever there is of us both!
Live on, remember us, and weep tears over my wound:
lover, do not shun the body of your lover.
You, I beg, obey the requests of the sister you loved too well!
I myself will obey our father's order.

What is interesting here, but is something the modern reader may
miss, is that the violent Aeolus, son of Helen, portrayed by Ovid is
diametrically opposite to the more benign Aeolus, son of Hippotas,

found in Homer's *Odyssey*, who had six daughters and six sons who he encouraged to marry each other. The two characters were often confused, though Ford has created a more benevolent father in Florio, and transferred to Giovanni the murderous possessiveness of Ovid's Aeolus. Not only might the idea of a blood-stained warning letter from a sister to her brother have suggested to Ford the letter Annabella writes in V.i, but he may have reworked other details, too: Canace's illness, the shrewdness of her Nurse reflected in the speed with which Putana recognizes the signs of pregnancy, or the brutal outbursts of Aeolus becoming Soranzo's violent responses to learning of the pregnancy (IV.iii). At the same time, the blade presented to Canace, her 'funeral gift' from her father, might have become the knife that traces the tragic route of Annabella's courtship, 'marriage' and death. Aeolus's wish that he who sent the dagger might see her death, 'and the eyes of its author contemplate the act' are seemingly transformed by Ford, with Giovanni playing the role of Aeolus, and not only witnessing, but perpetrating, the act itself, and so becoming the murderer of the baby. The story of Canace continued to inspire writers, such as Sperone Speroni, a Paduan philosopher and writer, whose verse tragedy *Canace et Macareo*, based on Ovid's version, appeared in 1546, and has been suggested as a possible influence on Ford. The play was the subject of much adverse criticism, received only one performance, and prompted debates on tragedy and the morality of the theatre. Although the characters do invoke the sympathy of the audience, in almost all other respects it is completely unlike Ford's play. There is no record of an English translation, and although someone might have read it to him, there is no evidence that Ford was sufficiently skilled in Italian to have read it otherwise.

Roper notes that another, though less well-known story of incest, found in Parthenius's *Erotica*, not only focuses on the brother, Leucippus, but also on the moment of the revelation of the incest, not found in Ovid or Rosset. The story was published in English in 1624, not long before the play's likely composition, in a compilation by Thomas Heywood which also includes the story of Canace. Roper favours Heywood's version as Ford's source, as in addition to narrative detail, it also includes the suggestion that 'want of action, in a stirring brain, and body, wrought this distemperature' in Leucippus's behaviour (rather than the curse of Aphrodite as in Parthenius's original) which might have appealed to Ford's interest in melancholic states of mind in addition to its more obvious dramatic potential.

## Medieval incest

Elizabeth Archibald observes that while classical and early modern texts often focused on the theme of incest, 'no other period can rival the Middle Ages for unblinking acceptance of many varieties of incest... as materials for tales of "sentence and solace"' (2002: 18). Medieval writers drew extensively on classical mythology for stories of incestuous relationships, although the stories of Oedipus' marriage to his mother (though unwitting and so not a carnal sin) or of Myrrha, who fell in love with her father and had a child, Adonis, by him were less popular sources than the story of Canace. In medieval responses to that story we find outright horror, such as Chaucer's Man of Law's description of incest as 'unkind abominations' ('unkind' used with exactly the same double-meaning – 'unnatural'/'unbrotherly' – that Annabella does at V.v.93). But in Gower's *Confessio Amantis* we encounter a more understanding reaction in which by stressing Canace's deep and genuine love for her brother, Gower 'does not condone the incest, but neither does he condemn it' (Archibald 2002: 21), but reserves his criticism for the wrathful father, Aeolus.

Two other stories of incest, popular in the Middle Ages, were undoubtedly known to Ford, though neither is a direct influence on this play: the story of Appollonius of Tyre (which in Gower's version was a source for Shakespeare's *Pericles*) and that of the relationship between Arthur and his (unrecognized) half-sister, Morgause, that produces a son, Mordred, which was told in Sir Thomas Malory's enormously popular epic *Le Morte d'Arthur*, which appeared in print in 1485.

## Rank and social conflict

Despite the fact that it only occupies around a third of the total running time, the majority of performances and critical responses to *'Tis Pity* have focused on the incestuous relationship of Annabella and Giovanni and, in particular, the balance between approval and criticism in Ford's treatment of the characters. Moreover, the plots that surround this core action have also been discussed largely from the perspective of their relationship to the Annabella–Giovanni thread, while with one or two exceptions, discussion of the characters who populate these plots has centred on their function in being, by comparison, so much less 'honourable' than Annabella and Giovanni that they serve to support a more sympathetic view of the lovers than would otherwise be possible.

In the Prologue to *The Lady's Trial* (1639) Ford contrasts himself with writers 'who idly scan affairs of state', and it is true that he was clearly not as interested in contemporary politics as, say, Massinger. Nevertheless, Clifford Leech was right to observe that Ford's 'view of society was intensely class-conscious', although his plays would seem to contradict Leech's follow-up point that Ford's 'ideal human being... was in essence a courtier who would win King Charles's praise', 1957: 122). Social historians have observed the theme of class hostility in plays of the 1620s and 1630s, but interpreted this as a dramatic convention, and they are not alone. Kathleen McLuskie, for example, is just one of Ford's critics (many of them, as she is herself, admirers of the playwright) who, while acknowledging the off-stage tensions circulating in Ford's society and fully aware of how some contemporary dramatists addressed these directly in their plays, nevertheless considers that 'Ford was primarily a purveyor of theatrical pleasures and offers no direct access to the real social tensions of this time' (1986: 124). Such a response implies that Ford is only interested in individual men and women who find their personal desires in conflict with the moral imperatives of the world around them. To an extent, of course, this is a fair assessment of his work, including collaborations, but it overlooks the care with which Ford creates a web of social and political pressures and how these impact on the 'dilemmas...grievances, anxieties and frustrations' (Butler 1984: 281) of his characters *and* his audience. And that audience, it is vital to remember, in the indoor playhouses was, if not as wide-ranging as in the outdoor playhouses, still a *heterogeneous* one, as the appeals made to different sections of that audience confirm (see p. 16). And of particular concern to both merchant and aristocrat was the question of marriage.

Throughout the play, reference is made by characters themselves or by others to their current or aspirant social status. Hippolita, for example, stung by Soranzo's rejection points out both that her own

birth 'was nobler and by much more free' than Annabella's, who she
cuttingly dismisses as 'goodly Madame Merchant' (II.ii.50, 48). As if to
justify his dismissal of any real justice in Parma, the Cardinal reminds
the citizens that Grimaldi is 'no common man, but nobly born',
indeed 'Of prince's blood', but that despite this Florio, though himself
only from the merchant class, 'Thought him too mean a husband' for
his daughter (III.ix.56−8). And, Putana, identifying the pros and cons
of Soranzo as a suitor, tops off her list by reminding Annabella that
he is 'more than all this, a nobleman' (I.ii.88). As a theme, exogamy
(marrying outside one's class) has frequently emerged throughout
English drama at times of perceived instability and porosity between
traditional class divisions (it is central to *Look Back in Anger*, for
example, set in the fluid society of post-war Britain). An upsurge in
class-crossing marriages occurred in the 1620s and 1630s, bringing 'a
degree of mingling between the peerage and the city without parallel
before and after' (Stone 1965: 632), and it was a social reality reflected
in a wide range of comic and serious plays, including *The Changeling*,
*Women Beware Women*, *A New Way to Pay Old Debts*, *The Roman Actor* and
*The Duchess of Malfi*. Lisa Hopkins is right to identify Ford as primarily
'a dramatist of the heart' (2010: 2), but the social body that surrounds
those hearts is a key factor in *'Tis Pity* too.

## Execution, anatomy and the theatre

'I had rather Chirurgeons' [Surgeons] Hall should beg my dead body for an
anatomy than thou beg my life.' (William Barksted and Lewis Machin, *The
Insatiate Countess*, V.ii.78−80)

The Phoenix playhouse in Drury Lane had two 'hidden' but important associations with other places of 'performance' popular in early
modern London, connections which as part of the contemporary
'culture of dissection' (Sawday 1995: ix) are especially relevant to
Ford's play. The first lay in the theatre's origins as a cockpit, where
two male birds fought each other, often to the death, an image that
resonates with both the general male competitiveness in the play
and with specific scenes such as the near-fight between Vasques and
Grimaldi in I.ii. The second, more important association is with the
anatomy theatres, 'the playhouses of organized violence' as Sawday

calls them (1995: ix). Indeed, in 1636, the architect Inigo Jones (at one time credited as the designer of the Phoenix) was responsible for a new anatomy theatre built at the Barber Surgeons' Hall in London, and his designs for that were bound together in the Worcester College collection with the drawings (not by Jones) for the playhouse. It is a resonant proximity for *'Tis Pity* demonstrates a web of associations with the act of anatomizing of the individual, explored metaphorically in the literary motif of the 'blazon' which is especially significant in its relation to this play given Giovanni's ultimate act of physical 'blazoning' by dissecting Annabella's body to remove one of its hidden, but most significant, elements- her heart. The connection between the blazon and the science and practice of contemporary anatomy is a crucial but complex one. As David Norbrook has written: 'the vogue in the sixteenth century for the blazon, the detailed enumeration of the parts of the woman's body, can be seen as reflecting the new scientific mentality with its mastering gaze, its passion for mapping the world in order *to gain power over it*' (Norbrook and Woudhuysen, 1992: 43; emphasis added). This association of the blazon with male power is also explored by Jonathan Sawday, who suggests that, metaphorically, 'female body parts were held aloft as tokens of intellectual mastery' with the English blazon in particular, 'partition[ing] the female body within an atmosphere which was... erotically charged' (1995: 197) an image that captures the struggle between Giovanni and Soranzo for ownership of Annabella's heart, in the recurrent verbal references to exposing the heart as a means of discovering the 'truth' of a person's intentions, and with the metaphor finally made flesh with Giovanni's 'dissection' of his sister's body. In this, Ford's work shares much with John Donne's poetry, such as the opening lines of *The Damp*, published in his *Songs and Sonnets* in 1633, the same year as *'Tis Pity*:

> When I am dead, and Doctors know not why,
> And my friends' curiosity
> Will have me cut up to survey each part,
> When they shall find your picture in my heart...

One further bleak, complicating layer of association, given that Annabella is 'guilty' of incest, is that the bodies used for anatomy experiments were those of executed criminals.

A classic example of the *blazon*, parodied by Shakespeare in Sonnet 130, is Thomas Watson's *The Hekatompathia, or Passionate Century of Love* (1581):

> Hark you that list to hear what saint I serve:
> Her yellow locks exceed the beaten gold,
> Her sparkling eyes in heav'n a place deserve,
> Her forehead high and fair, of comely mould.
>      Her words are music all of silver sound,
>      Her wit so sharp as like can scarce be found.
> Her eyebrow hangs like Iris in the skies,
> Her eagle's nose is straight of stately frame,
> On either cheek a rose and lily lies,
> Her breath is sweet perfume, or holy flame.
>      Her lips more red than coral stone,
>      Her neck more white than aged swans that moan.
> Her breast transparent is, like crystal rock,
> Her fingers long, fit for Apollo's lute,
> Her slipper such as Momus dare not mock,
> Her virtues all so great as make me mute.
>      What other parts she hath I need not say,
>      Whose face alone is cause of my decay.

## Melancholy, lovesickness and Neoplatonism

> Deep in a dump Jack Ford alone was got,
> With folded arms and melancholy hat.

These lines from William Heminges's *Elegy on Randolph's Finger* are one of the very few contemporary references to the playwright, but the image they conjure up not only chimes exactly with the picture of a lover on the frontispiece of Robert Burton's *The Anatomy of Melancholy* (1621), but also the less often remarked on word 'alone' reflects Florio's description of his distracted, lovesick son, 'so devoted to his book' (I.iii.5). *The Anatomy of Melancholy* (published under the pseudonym Democritus Junior) is a vast and sometimes rambling discourse on virtually all aspects of human behaviour, with examples drawn from a bewildering range of contemporary and classical literary, philosophical and medical sources. In Book III, Burton turns his attention to Love, seeking to distinguish between Platonic love – a noble love which 'inflames our souls with a divine heat ... elevates to

God… and reconciles us unto him' – and what Burton terms 'heroical love' or lovesickness', which is 'a frequent cause of melancholy, and deserves much rather to be called burning lust'. It 'infects' and 'depresses' the soul of man, causes 'cares and troubles' and 'deforms our life', whereas noble love 'cleanseth' the soul, brings us 'quietness of mind' and 'informs' our lives.

> The love of God begets the love of man, and by this love of our neighbour, the love of God is nourished and increased. By this happy union of love, all well-governed families and cities are combined, the heavens annexed, and divine souls complicated, the world itself composed, and all that is in it conjoined in God and reduced to one. This love causeth true and absolute virtues, the life and spirit and root of every virtuous action, it finisheth prosperity, easeth adversity, corrects all natural encumbrances, inconveniences, sustained by Faith and Hope, which with this our love make an indissoluble twist, a Gordian knot, an equilateral triangle. And yet the greatest of them is love, which inflames our souls with a divine heat, and being so inflamed purgeth, and so purged elevates to God, makes an atonement and reconciles us unto him. That other [heroical] love infects the soul of man; this cleanseth, that depresseth; this creates, that causeth cares and troubles; this quietness of mind, this informs, that deforms our life, that leads to repentance, this to heaven.
>
> … But to enlarge or illustrate this power and effects of love, is to set a candle in the sun. It rageth amongst all sorts and conditions of men, but it is most evident amongst such as are young and lusty, in the flower of their years, nobly descended, high fed, and such as live idle and at ease, and for that cause which our Divines call lust, or this mad and beastly passion, as I have said, is called by our Physicians, Heroical love… because noble men make a common practise of it, and are so commonly affected with it [and it is by others defined as] a disease or melancholy vexation or anguish of mind, in which a man continually meditates of the beauty, gesture, manners of his mistress, and troubles himself about it. And [he] desires… with all intention and eagerness of mind to compass or enjoy her. As melancholy hunters trouble themselves about their sports, the covetous their gold and goods, so is he tormented still about his mistress…. Tully calls it a furious disease of the mind, Plato madness itself, Ficinus a species of madness, Rhases a melancholy passion, and most physicians make it a species, or kind of melancholy…. But properly it is a passion of the brain, as all other melancholy, by reason of corrupt imagination, and [as]… both imagination and reason are misaffected, because of his corrupt judgement, and continual meditation of that which he desires, he may truly be said to be melancholy.

As Dawson points out, however, this binary classification of positive and negative obscures the fact that these apparent opposites
identified by Burton were understood by contemporaries often to
co-exist, the tension so created leading to extreme and defining
states of consciousness (2008: 129). Some critics of Ford who see
him as having too much sympathy with the sexual behaviour of his
characters explain the playwright's lapse of moral judgement by his
adherence to a Neoplatonic view of love and sex.

Neoplatonism is a term applied to the philosophical and religious
writings initially of a group of Italian writers of the fifteenth and
sixteenth centuries, based on the work of the Greek philosopher
Plato, in which they sought to fuse classical and Christian ideas, and
whose work focused on the opposition between the corporeal and
the spiritual, a concept derived from Plato's distinction between the
'idea' and its material existence. Their ideas were introduced into
England via the work of continental writers and visits by leading
Neoplatonists such as Erasmus. Although Neoplatonism was never
as popular or widespread in England as on the Continent, it became
especially fashionable in the late 1620s to early 1630s with the cult of
Platonic love encouraged at court by Queen Henrietta Maria, wife
of Charles I. In theory, as James Howell described it in 1634, Platonic
love was physical, but consisted of 'contemplation and ideas of the
mind, not in any carnal fruition', and, noting (with an implication of
its propriety) that 'there will be a masque shortly of it, whereof her
majesty and her Maids of Honour will be a part' (quoted in Dawson
2008: 138; spelling modernized). However, attitudes to Neoplatonism
veered between those who praised it and celebrated it, to those who
derided it, arguing that true love could not and should not separate
spiritual and physical emotion and feeling, and, where the concept
was used as a seduction technique, an example of court hypocrisy. A
number of significant critical works on 'Tis Pity (e.g, by Sensabaugh
(1944), Oliver (1055), Stavig (1968); see Chapter 6) have addressed the
play's relationship to the concept of Platonic love. Others, such as
Kauffman, Bueler and Forker argue that Giovanni's single-minded
pursuit of his desire results in a love which Giovanni may consider
to be 'like religious mystery' and justifiably lead to 'sacrificial rite',
whereas his behaviour 'is seen by the sane… as madness, depravity
[and] monstrous egotism' (Forker 1990: 167). Dawson, however, argues
for the need to see the interrelation between Giovanni's Platonism and

what she terms his 'narcissism', as Ford offers a 'complex vision of the way in which these discourses intertwine', developing the notion inherent in Neoplatonism of a 'spiritual resemblance between lovers' that 'allowed for the narcissistic mirroring of the lover in the ennobled object of desire (2008: 141), an idea dramatized, for example, in the moment where Annabella describes a young man she does not recognize but obviously finds attractive as having the 'blessed shape / Of some celestial creature' (I.ii.127–8), only to discover he is, in fact, her brother. These issues become especially significant where the subject matter concerns the incestuous love of brother and sister where blood-relationship, normally the obstacle to a sexual relationship, becomes a key aspect of the erotic desire felt by the lovers. As explored in Chapter 2, Giovanni's narcissism is revealed from the play's opening scene, as he pursues the Neoplatonic argument that similarities between a man and woman generate love to an extreme, by including the 'one womb' and blood-ties he and Annabella share. In his essay, 'Brother–Sister Incest', David Bergeron notes that for Annabella, Giovanni 'is a mirror by which and through which she perceives her love for him: each reflects the other' (1986: 212), an idea that is fully dramatized in the wooing in I.ii, as Giovanni argues that in resembling each other physically they also 'share one beauty to a double soul' (233), and then, even more powerfully, when, kneeling face to face, they exactly mirror each other's words, gestures and feelings (248–54).

# 4    Key Productions and Performances

The life of these things consists in Action. (John Marston, 1604)

'Tis Pity remained in the repertoire of Christopher Beeston's company until his death in 1638, and was then included in the plays protected by the Lord Chamberlain for Christopher's son, William, who succeeded his father as manager of the Phoenix playhouse (see pp. 5–9) where he ran the King and Queen's Young Company. All the London commercial playhouses were closed by Order of Parliament in 1642, but 'Tis Pity was among the first plays to be revived when they reopened following the restoration of Charles II. On 9 September 1661, the avid play-goer Samuel Pepys, after lunching rather too well ('I drank so much wine that I was not fit for business'), 'walked in Westminster Hall awhile, and thence to Salisbury Court playhouse, where was acted the first time [i.e. since the theatres re-opened] 'Tis Pity She's a Whore, a simple play and ill-acted'. Pepys's disappointment was mitigated by the presence of a 'most pretty and ingenious lady' sitting near him, but it is especially frustrating for us that he failed to record exactly who he saw perform the play, as this production featured the first women to play the female roles but who these actresses were is not known. The company at Salisbury Court was led by George Jolly, who in 1662 took his company out of London to tour its repertory of pre-Interregnum plays, and there is a record, though no detail, of a performance of 'Tis Pity at the King's Arms in Norwich later that year. However, responses throughout the eighteenth and nineteenth centuries to the content of the play, and in particular to Ford's handling of his material (see Chapter 6) helped keep 'Tis Pity off the stage for another 250 years, until it was revived in November 1894 in Paris.

# Ford in France

Ford's play had already been praised by the influential French critic Hippolyte Taine, in a collection of essays published in 1864. To Taine, unlike almost all the English critics who preceded and indeed followed him (see Chapter 6, *passim*), the most praiseworthy thing about the play was precisely its presentation of the 'irresistible love which falls on [the lovers], the ancient love of Pasiphae or Myrrha [incestuous lovers in classical literature; see p. 98], a kind of madness, a spell to which everything must succumb'. Taine particularly admired IV.iii, V.v and V.vi, concluding that 'tragedy has no where left to go after that'. The 1894 production of *'Tis Pity* was presented at the Théâtre de l'Oeuvre in an adaptation, titled (significantly) *Annabella*, by the Belgian poet, playwright, essayist and (in 1911) Nobel Prize winner Maurice Maeterlinck, and directed by Aurelien Lugné-Poe (who also played Giovanni). Lugné-Poe is likely to have known of Taine's enthusiasm for the play, but a more immediate encouragement to produce it was a letter he received from Marcel Schwob, the French writer (who delivered a lecture on the play before curtain-up on the opening night), pressing upon the director the merits of this 'extraordinary play', while insisting that it would take a poet to provide a successful translation. Maeterlinck was chosen and accepted the commission for, although he had understandable reservations about the reception the play's subject matter might receive (and which, as Roper suggests, may account for his 'greatly softened' adaptation), he himself had a perceptive and sympathetic response to it and to Ford, who he described in his introduction to the published text as 'the most profound feminist of the Shakespearean age'. To Maeterlinck, 'the love of brother for sister, viewed from a standpoint sufficiently lofty, is a crime against morality, but not against human nature; and there is at least some measure of palliation in the youth of the pair, and in the passion that blinds them', but while the play dramatized the 'violence and passion of incestuous love', it also showed the 'forces *beneath* and *behind* the action' (McGuiness, 2000: 44).

The production received a mixed reception. The critic of *Le Temps* wrote that 'To my mind, the interpretation has falsified the sense of [the play]' and criticized Lugné-Poe and Berthe Bady (Annabella) for acting with 'hands in pretty gestures, eyes turned to the sky, an air of mysticism, a slow walk, light, monotonous voice, like saints descended from a Giotto fresco' (7 November 1894), none of which seems suited to Ford's play. The reviewer for the *New York Times* was especially blunt: 'It is very long, very tedious and very dull.... Ford's play is useless, and should have been left to dust and mice' (18 November 1894). In fact, *'Tis Pity* has remained reasonably popular on the Parisian stage, with professional productions in 1933, 1961, 1975 (twice), 1983, 1987, 1992 and, in 1997 at the Théâtre National Populaire, adapted (into prose) and directed by Jérôme Savary. Maeterlinck's influence remains strong, with the lengthy programme notes for Savary's production quoting him extensively.

Before moving to consider productions in the United Kingdom, I want to touch briefly on a production of the play which remained only in the imagination of its creator, Antonin Artaud, but whose ideas about it have not only influenced critical writings on the play but also later stagings. In 1921, the 25-year-old Artaud was introduced to Lugné-Poe and for a short time became an actor at the Théâtre de l'Oeuvre (where Lugné-Poe had staged Ford's play in 1894). Artaud's own dramatic work shows not only the formal and tonal influences of the Jacobean drama, but also – in *The Cenci* and *The Spurt of Blood*, for example – shares an interest in the theme of incest. Artaud was also an admirer of Maeterlinck, whose version of *'Tis Pity* led him to find in Ford's ability to portray the most extreme passions and passionate acts an example of the kind of theatre Artaud himself wished to create. In his essay 'Theatre and the Plague', Artaud wrote that 'If we desire an example of absolute freedom in revolt, Ford's Annabella provides this poetic example bound up with the image of absolute danger', and he imagined a performance of *'Tis Pity* (1970: 19–20) in which, as the audience approach the end of the play, telling themselves 'there must be retribution and death for such boldness and for such an irresistible crime':

> Giovanni, the lover, inspired by a great impassioned poet, places himself above retribution and crime by a kind of indescribably passionate crime, places himself above threats, above horror by an even greater horror that baffles both law and morals and those who dare to set themselves up as judges. A clever trap is laid; orders are given for a great banquet where henchmen and hired assassins hide among the guests, ready to pounce on him at the first sign. But this lost, hunted hero inspired by love, will not allow anyone to judge this love.

Artaud's vision of the play, and in particular this climactic scene, has clearly influenced later critical writings (especially those who see Giovanni as an 'existential hero'; see p. 141), but significantly, by seeing Giovanni as he sees himself, and praising his self-determination while ignoring his denial of any such freedom to Annabella, Artaud also influenced the portrayal of the character on stage as a 'heroic' figure.

## Ford in Britain

In Britain, there was to be no revival until the aptly named Phoenix Society produced the play as its fourteenth production, at the Shaftesbury Theatre, London, on the evening of Sunday, 28 January 1923, and again the following afternoon. The Phoenix Society had been formed in 1919 with the express purpose of reviving neglected plays from the sixteenth to the eighteenth centuries, and was in effect a theatre club, with performances confined to its subscribers, so allowing it to circumvent the regulations on what could be presented on stage. The critic of *The Times* (30 January 1923) considered that the production 'passed over the evil of the blood-relationship between Giovanni and Annabella', observing that in their love 'there is no shadow of perversion… a proud love… without guilt'. However, the slightly odd reference to 'the beautiful death of Annabella' and suggestion that the last scene was a means only of bringing the play to an end as if Ford had lost interest in it might have been a result of the 'very slight alterations' of the text noted by Davril (1954: 499–500). The reviewer was critical of the smaller parts, for whom Ford 'cared nothing', though he praised the actors who played them, apart from Michael Sherbrooke who he clearly thought overacted: 'we were given little chance to think of Giovanni and Annabella when Vasques was on the stage'. In the *New Statesman* (3 February 1923), Desmond McCarthy praised many of the performances, but regretted that the production lost something of the 'barbaric ferocity' of the original, in particular the climax of the play which, perhaps in response to the sensitivities of a modern audience, lacked the sadistic, but integral, horror of the original. Equally perceptively, McCarthy, unlike many critics, also acknowledged that while the audience laughed, the death of 'that fluttering fool' Bergetto 'is far more moving than the deaths of the noble, tragic characters'.

The next performances of the play were also ostensibly private, when it was staged at the Arts Theatre Club in London on 30 December 1934 and 6 January 1935, with a further performance on 13 January. Despite the good box-office, it was generally poorly received, though criticism was levelled more at the production than the play itself. A typewritten review signed 'C.L.', (Charles Landstone, and probably written for the *Jewish Chronicle*), found in the copy of the programme held in the University of Bristol Theatre Collection, records that he was 'profoundly moved' by the 'sweeping grandeur and terror' of the story of the 'incestuous passion' of Annabella and Giovanni. *The Times* reviewer (anticipating a recurrent theme in criticism of productions) accepted that 'there is a good deal to be said for the experiment of a realistic performance of Ford's play, even one so realistic that it runs to what appears to be a genuine, and is certainly a dripping, heart at the end of Giovanni's dagger', but queried whether 'an excess of realism might overshoot the mark', arguing that 'the artificiality of poetry is needed to make such events reasonable, and the performances must emphasise the poetry rather than the mere record of bizarre emotions', finding 'the quieter, the most obviously poetical, passages' the most successful.

It was not until 1940 that the first *public*, commercial production of *'Tis Pity* was staged in Britain since the 1660s, when it was presented by Donald Wolfit and Company for what turned out to be just two performances at the Cambridge Arts Theatre on 13 May, before staging it again, at the Strand Theatre, London, the following year. Wolfit had been invited to perform four plays at Cambridge by the economist, Bursar of King's College and founder of the Cambridge Arts Theatre Maynard Keynes (who was a champion of neglected early modern drama). Wolfit chose *Hamlet* and *The Merchant of Venice* as the Shakespeare plays, followed by *Volpone*. For the fourth play, Wolfit 'ultimately settled on John Ford's great tragedy *'Tis Pity She's a Whore*' which, alert to the play's potential to shock, he sent to Keynes to read. He received the following response:

> It is a wonderfully strong piece of work, which needs doing with gusto and in the Italian manner. But I had not realised that the theme was so exclusively incest without mitigation or remorse. Clearly it is strong meat for the general public. On the other hand, the title, fortunately perhaps, is calculated to warn the public. (Wolfit 1954: 196)

Understandably, Wolfit remained apprehensive about how the play would be received, and was particularly concerned whether the Lord Chamberlain's office (responsible until 1968 for approving and, where it thought necessary, censoring plays prior to performance) would issue a licence. He was therefore delighted to learn that as *'Tis Pity* had been first performed before the Theatres Act of 1843 it was classed as an 'old play', which meant the Lord Chamberlain had no jurisdiction over it *unless* – Wolfit was even more surprised to discover – they made any cuts or revisions, in which case they *would* have to submit it. Wolfit responded that it was his intention 'to play it in full and, as the subject matter of the play deals with incest' noting that 'although the verse and the treatment raise it to the greatest heights of poetry and drama, [we] counted ourselves most fortunate in this decision' (1954: 196).

Wolfit devised a permanent setting vaguely reminiscent of the original performance space: an upper level for the bed chamber, a central entrance for the street scenes and a 'pillared alcove' which by pulling a traverse curtain could become a private space such as the Friar's cell. All these scenic elements were painted black, with a cyclorama of an Italian sky and the outline shapes of the cypress trees typical of northern Italy. The critic Audrey Williamson praised the performances of Wolfit and Rosalind Iden (his wife, playing Annabella), especially for how they 'caught the iridescent fire of the love scenes and the verse', but thought the production 'stressed the melodrama at times to the point of laughter', dismissing Giovanni's final scene with the dagger as merely a 'shocking concession to the groundling's taste for horror (the more shocking since it is entirely unnecessary to the plot)' (Williamson 1951: 281–2; in fact, as an indoor play, it was not seen by the 'groundlings'). Although the production was generally well received, and broke the long-standing taboo on its public production, after two performances protests resulted in the production's closure.

It was another 20 years before the play was performed again professionally: 1955, at the Nottingham Playhouse. Since then, however, in comparison with Ford's other plays and those of his contemporaries, it has been revived reasonably frequently in the UK, with (up until 2011) 13 major professional productions, as well as countless fringe, amateur and student presentations. (See the New Mermaid edition for a partial list of productions up to 1999.) In addition, the play has

been heard on radio – a major contributor to the revival of interest
in Jacobean drama – three times, and seen three times on screen (see
Chapter 5).

The early 1970s was a particularly active period for the revival of
early modern plays by writers other than Shakespeare, with three
productions of *The Duchess of Malfi* in 1970–1, and two of *'Tis Pity* in
1972: by the Actors' Company, directed by David Giles and by the
National Theatre Touring Company, directed by Roland Joffé who,
eight years later, would direct the play for television (see pp. 127–32).
Giles's production was set in the Edwardian period, with overtones
of the Mafia world (a common motif in revivals at this time, popularized by Francis Ford Coppola's *The Godfather*, 1972). Reviewing Joffé's
production, Irving Wardle identified precisely those aspects of the
play that performance can often reveal more clearly than reading,
and so challenge the obsession with the sibling lovers and complaints
about the play's structure and tonal shifts that had for centuries
dominated non-performance based criticism (see Chapter 6):

> *'Tis Pity* is famed for the incestuous central relationship of Giovanni and
> Isabella; but in actual playing time this counts for no more than the clown-
> ish courtship of Bergetto and the two interlocking revenge sub-plots. As
> far as mechanics go, there are few Jacobean plays in the same class; and
> Ford also possesses the uncharacteristic qualities of genuinely comic
> funny scenes and... social complexity.... The power of money, of aristoc-
> racy, of papal authority come over with corresponding weight. (*The Times*,
> 3 August 1972)

The production (in keeping with the play itself) 'refused to slant
the play either for or against the lovers, the church, the commercial
world, or indeed any of the groups of characters; instead, one aspect
of society counterbalanced another' (Warren, 1988: 12). Other aspects
of the production were less successful. It is not uncommon for male
roles in early modern plays to be played as female roles, but here
the opposite was the case, with Putana becoming a male 'giggling,
nudging blabbermouth' (*The Times*, 3 August 1972).

## Royal Shakespeare Company, the Other Place, Stratford-upon-Avon, 1977

The Other Place (its name taken from *Hamlet*, IV.iii.35) opened in
1974, the brainchild of Trevor Nunn, then the RSC's Artistic Director,

who had become convinced of the particular qualities that a small, intimate space could bring to the production of early modern plays, and whose 1976 production of *Macbeth* had further convinced him, audiences and critics, of the rare degree of intimacy and engagement with the performance it allowed.*Tis Pity* was directed by Ron Daniels (his first classical play for the company), with Barbara Kellerman (Annabella), Simon Rouse (Giovanni), Nigel Terry (Soranzo), Geoffrey Hutchings (Vasques) and Matthew Guiness (Friar). Its setting (Chris Dyer) and costumes (Jenny Beavan) evoked both the 1920s and 1970s and, as in Joffe's production, suggested Mafia resonances. It also stressed the religious context of the play, with a set dominated by a large crucifix and statue of the Virgin Mary. It opened with an interpolated scene as the Cardinal said Mass, and later introduced a wedding Mass at the opening of IV.i. Although not played as adolescents, Annabella and Giovanni 'had the simplicity of children' (Warren, 1988: 15) that effected a powerful contrast with the explicit portrayal of their sexual relationship: II.i was played with the couple naked in bed, excited and joyous after their love-making. Unlike later productions on screen (see Chapter 5), and, I think, truer to the text (see pp. 79–81), Annabella was confused and frightened at the moment of her death, unable to read Giovanni's shifting behaviour. Most significantly (and less true to Ford in my view), Giovanni was presented as an existential hero, the influence of Artaud not invoked but clearly present in Ron Daniels's view of the character which in my opinion saw Giovanni, uncritically, as he sees himself. Critics found the crucial, and complex, relationship between Soranzo and Vasques underpowered, but the production offered an affecting relationship between Poggio and Bergetto (essential to the proper working of III. vii and the overall moral compass of the play), aided by directorial additions such as leaving Poggio alone on stage at the end of III. ix, shaking the gates of the Cardinal's palace in sorrow and anger. Moments such as this, and that at the end of III.vii, in Dessen's words, 'realized the function of such a subordinate action in such a tragedy' (1986: 93), and provided a convincing argument to those critics who dismiss Ford's sub-plots as intrusive (see pp. 142–6).

## Citizens Theatre, Glasgow, 1988

> HENRY:   Anyway, I thought you were committing incest in Glasgow.
> ANNIE:   I haven't said I'll do it.

HENRY: I think you should. It's classy stuff, Webster. I love all that Jacobean sex and violence.

ANNIE: It's Ford, not Webster. It's Elizabethan not Jacobean. (Tom Stoppard, *The Real Thing*, Act Two, Scene Five)

Annie may have got her dating a bit wrong, but Stoppard's 1982 play anticipated the Glasgow Citizens' production by six years. (See Wilkinson, 2010: 53–5 for a shrewd analysis of Stoppard's use of *'Tis Pity*.) The director/designer Philip Prowse set the entire play in a vast, black and white cathedral, its walls hung with religiously inflected erotic paintings. As if expanding Ford's description of the setting for III.vi, no fewer than three altars dominated the stage, shrouded in black and lit by candles and flickering red sanctuary lamps. To complete the sensory experience, censers pushed out the heavy, heady scent of incense while bells of different weights rang throughout the play, to give both background atmosphere and to point up particular moments in the action. Coffins, some draped in blood-stained sheets, replaced benches, with the implications of 'plague and battle taking their unseen toll on the city' (*Financial Times*, 22 February 1988), with the death imagery continued in the canopy decorated with skulls and crucifix that formed the head of the lovers' bed that dominated the upstage area. Three mobile linen-covered screens allowed a more intimate space to be created for the scenes between the lovers. In common with other Citizens Theatre productions, visual elaboration was matched by sweeping changes to the text. Firmly in line with the setting, the role of the Cardinal was expanded to embrace much of the role of Donado, whose character was cut, while also taking over aspects of the role of Florio, who became the siblings' mother, Floria. In I.ii, for example, it was the Cardinal who broke up the fight between Grimaldi and Vasques with the reallocated and rewritten line, 'What mean these sudden broils within my church' (21). Richardetto and Philotis were also cut, so thinning the role of Grimaldi and the context of Hippolita's revenge. Bergetto (with his uncle Donado gone) became both the nephew of the Cardinal and, by cutting all the character's lines, 'a crippled religious inmate, a mute penitent in the train of the Cardinal, gibbering words ceaselessly at the Stations of the Cross (*Financial Times*). As a result, the complex responses an audience has to the death of Bergetto in III.vii were lost, the scene moving directly from 'How is't

Bergetto? Slain? It cannot be! / Are you sure y'are hurt' (now spoken by Grimaldi) to Floria speaking Richardetto's 'Give me a light. What's here? All blood'.

For the critic of the *Sunday Times*, the result of Prowse's cutting was that the audience got 'not so much an ornate English baroque drama as a clean, hard Spanish renaissance tragedy [though he doesn't actually name one], swifter, shorter and less self-indulgent than Ford's play', but in so doing lost the 'mix of bloody deeds and gruesome joviality that makes Jacobean tragedy so difficult to do' (28 February 1988). The horrors were not entirely skimped, however: a blood-covered, nearly naked Giovanni carried a 'real' heart, and the bodies of both Annabella and Putana were consigned to the flames of a bonfire in the church itself, underlining religion's role as the executor of revenge in the name of justice (and so avoiding the question of which 'woman' the Cardinal refers to at V.vi.132; see p. 86). The care with which the director's changes established a world of corruption in Parma suggested an interpretation that saw the illicit love of Annabella and Giovanni as innocent by comparison. As I have discussed in the Commentary, it seems to me Ford creates a greater equality of balance between the public and private worlds than that reading suggests, but it led here to particular focus on the portrayal of the incestuous lovers. Unsurprisingly, the responses of critics were divided. The review in the *Observer* found that the world surrounding the lovers matched the siblings, who were 'played as charmless and cool, she pallidly smiling, he arrogant and sour' (28 February 1988). Others too found the lovers' performances underpowered, especially Tristram Wymark's Giovanni. In *The Times*, he was described as 'a petulant, arrogant sub-Byronic boy... suggesting that, far from being in the grip of uncontrollable passion for [Annabella], he just invented the whole thing to draw attention to himself' (23 February 1988). The *Independent* saw him as a 'romantic rebel,... a Pre-Raphaelite youth with a sickly pallor' with both lovers lacking much in the way of 'psychological subtlety', appearing more as 'hapless pawns' (22 February 1988), unlike the self-determining characters found in the play. For Eric Shorter in the *Daily Telegraph* Wymark looked romantic, but by 'mumbling' throughout sounded as though the role was too much for him, while as Annabella, Yolanda Vasquez, was 'loud and graceless instead of sad and pathetic' (23 February 1988). More than one reviewer of Prowse's production drew attention to the 'newly timid and censorious' (*Financial Times*) mood of the UK in the late 1980s, 'a time when sexual love that is not socially sanctioned… is increasingly feared and hated', with films like *Fatal Attraction* savaging 'the lustful single woman' and society turning against homosexual love (*Guardian*, 22 February 1988). It was a climate in which while a theatre might hesitate to advertise to put the title of Ford's play on their posters, it was equally unsurprising that the play's theme, and Ford's treatment of it, would appeal to theatre makers. It was, therefore, with particular interest that a number of reviews of the Glasgow production looked forward to the production at the National Theatre in London, directed by the celebrated dramatist Alan Ayckbourn, which would start its preview performances less than a week later.

Ayckbourn's production, staged in the large space of the National's Olivier Theatre, was played on a setting suggesting the skyline of Parma. The lovers (Rupert Graves and Suzan Sylvester) were played as very young, with the result that that strand of the play most resembled a youth theatre production (an effect not helped by some less than convincing scene painting), and that by striving for youthfulness the actors lost the mature control of the verse that is required. (The result was not dissimilar to that created by Zeffirelli's casting of inexperienced actors in his film version of *Romeo and Juliet*.) By stressing their youth and innocence, the deviant nature of their passionate love – a complexity that Ford is at pains to maintain in balance – was lost.

### Royal Shakespeare Company, Swan Theatre, Stratford-upon-Avon, 1991

Audiences would have to wait only three years for the opportunity to see another major production of the play, when, in 1991, the RSC staged the play once more, this time in the Swan Theatre, directed by David Leveaux, who in the same season also directed *Romeo and Juliet* on the RSC main stage. The Swan had been opened in 1986 with the express purpose of allowing the RSC to stage the less well-known plays from the early modern and Restoration periods. The auditorium and stage replicate the basic arrangement of a Jacobean indoor playhouse: a thrust stage (deeper than would have been found at the Phoenix or Blackfriars) is surrounded by audiences on three sides, with the rear wall of the stage capable of having a gallery across it at the height of the first gallery of seating. There are entrances to the stage from the rear and through the auditorium on walkways to the down-stage corners of the stage. Leveaux and his designer, Kenny Miller, took advantage of the nature of the theatre to create a production that matched the likely simplicity of the first productions of the play, with a minimum of setting and properties, allowing the majority of scenes to flow without scene changes, so maintaining the driving energy of the action. The upper level was used too, not only in the scenes specified in the Quarto (I.ii, III.i and V.i) but also II.iv and III.ix). The setting was 1930s Italy. A particular feature of the production was the very low lighting levels, with the sequence of night scenes in Act III (see pp. 7–9) played at times virtually in the dark – in III.vi the deputy stage manager has written in the prompt copy a reminder to turn out even the lights in the control box to prevent any light spill into the auditorium. Music was used sparingly to bridge between some, but by no means all, scenes, and was a percussive 'musique concrète', often imitating what the prompt copy describes as a 'heartbeat'. The interval was placed after III.ix.

This production succeeded in capturing the fine balances in the play between criticism and approval for the incestuous lovers, helped by Jonathan Cullen's willingness not to seek the audience's acceptance of Giovanni's actions. In fact, the performances overall were universally strong, some outstanding. The text was played virtually intact, apart from a few words changed for ease of understanding. The only cut of any substance was the removal of Richardetto from the final scene, which allowed the momentum of the final moments to be played without the interruption of the revelation of his identity to the characters, but not the audience, who know it already and whose interest will rightly be on the Cardinal's shameful manoeuvrings. It was noticeable that the comic scenes were played almost in their entirety, trusting to the actors' skill to get the laughs, which they did without recourse to the annoying habit of underlining a potentially obscure line (especially if a sexual pun is suspected) with an enforcing gesture. In I.ii, for example, 'as long as they had either land or money left them to inherit' (108–9) was cut, whereas Bergetto's more likely-seeming candidate for excision – 'I have seen an ass and a mule trot the Spanish pavin with a better grace' (115–16) – survived and duly got a laugh. Roland Wymer notes that 'modern productions [provide] repeated and irrefutable evidence of the theatrical effectiveness of the minor characters' (1995: 131) suggesting that those academic critics who are quick to dismiss Ford's comic characters should try watching the text in the hands of truly skilful comic actors, as no doubt Ford's audience did. Some cuts, however, affected how Ford's text was clearly intended to work with its audience. In II.ii, for example, in the prompt copy, l. 141 ('Work you that way, old mole? Then I have the wind of you.') is crossed out, the effect of which is to remove our understanding that Vasques is fully aware that he is being manipulated, an understanding that was not replaced by the actor's performance, so reducing the complexity – and pleasure – in the scene. At the same time, earlier in the same scene, Soranzo's ferocity towards Hippolita – at one point grabbing her and throwing her violently to the ground – prefigured his behaviour to Annabella in IV.iii, so making it clear how his verbal anger could easily ignite into physical violence.

From the opening of the first scene, the Friar and Giovanni were matched in intensity (Giovanni flinging himself to the floor, in floods of tears; a number of critics compared him to Romeo), with the things that held them together being stressed as hard as the differences between them: the Friar's parting words to Giovanni – 'Away. / My blessing with thee.' – was clearly sincere, the stress on 'We' in 'We have need to pray' underlining his willingness to share with his pupil in the struggle ahead. Similar levels of passion infused the following scene, where weapons replace words. The machismo of the combatants was underscored, for example, when, as Grimaldi threatens Soranzo as he exits, Soranzo, in a sharp white suit that stood out from the dark of the other characters', stood before him, hands down, inviting him to stab: 'I fear thee not, Grimaldi' (I.ii.51). In his second scene with the Friar, Giovanni's manner was very different: confident now that his love has been returned, he taunted the Friar, relishing his victory, his feelings for his sister evoked in the powerfully poetic delivery of II.v.45–58. A number of parallels were employed to enforce ideas, such as Annabella with Hippolita, both victims of Soranzo's (and male) violence, or the loyal relationship between Bergetto and Poggio offering a comparison with the manoeuvrings and deceptions elsewhere.

By placing his production in a 'modern' setting, Leveaux was able to underline 'the timeless hypocrisy of the family, the Church and a

society that preaches one thing while practising plenty of the other'
(*Guardian*, 27 June 1991), the speed with which lives could be destroyed
neatly enforced by the staging: as plans are laid for a banquet to
draw Giovanni to his death, Soranzo's servant, Vasques (a brilliant
performance by Jonathan Hyde, shifting from amiability to hooded-
eyed cruelty in a second) deftly oversaw the turning of the lovers' bed
from V.v into a dining table, the crumpled sheets replaced by starched
cloth, and Giovanni's dagger by the best cutlery. And Cullen, entering
with Annabella's heart was completely drenched in blood, an image
that, in Kate Wilkinson's eyes, suggested that he had 'in some sense
had his own heart ripped out… underlining his love and grief for
his sister' (2010: 44), but which for me confirmed the sheer brutal
butchery of his final actions derived from the actor's interpretation
of Giovanni as, in Cullen's own words, a 'sexual terrorist' who denies
Annabella any of the 'freedom' Giovanni trumpets (private letter).

### West Yorkshire Playhouse, Leeds, 2011

In 2011 a 'sensationally, unmissably good' (*Daily Telegraph*, 19 May 2011)
production of *'Tis Pity* was staged at the West Yorkshire Playhouse
in Leeds. Even before its first night the production was embroiled
in a controversy over its poster, which set the play's title adjacent to
an image of the pièta, the dead Christ cradled in his mother's arms,
leading some to see an implicit association between the Virgin Mary
and 'Whore'. The Catholic Bishop of Leeds asked for the poster to
be withdrawn, and at one point rehearsals were interrupted by the
arrival at the theatre of the police, responding to complaints about
the image. The theatre pressed on, however, hanging a large banner
outside the building that read 'Judge the play, not the poster'. In the
event, apart from an ill-informed review in the *Guardian* the production, by Jonathan Munby, was widely praised in the local and national
press.

Set in stylish 1960s Italy, a society of 'lounge-suited menace'
(*Independent on Sunday*, 17 May 2011), the personal story of the illicit
relationship between brother and sister (played beautifully by two
young actors, Damien Molloy and Sara Vickers) was set clearly in the
wider context – at the end of I.ii, for example, Munby took advantage
of the large Courtyard Theatre stage to emphasize these two, small
figures, isolated from the world around them, their exit, laughing,

overlapping with the entrance of Florio and Donado, an image of the family and social pressures with which their relationship would soon have to contend – Florio, for example, despite a certain surface affability, clearly knew what he wanted and would get it. Similarly, in II.i, the sexual nature of the siblings' relationship was made explicit, with the naked couple sharing (a nice touch) a single-bed, their words of love backed by the chiming of the church bell, a reminder of the religious opposition they will face. Some directorial decisions further underlined the sexual dynamics of the play, such as setting II.ii in Soranzo's bedroom rather than his study, others sought to iron out plot elements that the director considered more complicating than resonant, such as making Richardetto a real doctor, and removing the plot-element of him being Hippolita's 'lost' husband. Bergetto was doubled with the Cardinal, and Poggio was cut completely.

The test of updating a play is the degree to which the process results in a texture different from, but every bit as rich as the original, and in this respect the production was especially successful. For example, Bergetto rode a Vespa scooter on stage, and at the opening of IV.i, Hippolita (Sally Dexter), here dressed ominously in black rather than ironically in white, crooned the sixties Burt Bacharach hit, 'Anyone Who Had a Heart', its effect rightly 'hilarious and disquieting in equal measure' (The Independent on Sunday, 17 May 2011). The text was cut and altered during the rehearsal period, often to try to iron out seeming inconsistencies in the narrative: for example, wanting to keep the overall pace of the play's action, and troubled by Ford's reference to 'nine months space' (V.vi.44), the director made it 'nine days' (private email), and other slight changes made to give a clearer sense of why Richardetto (now no longer with a personal revenge motive) should be willing to help Grimaldi kill Soranzo.

The stage setting (Mike Britton) was especially effective, scenic elements moving on trucks or being flown to shift location swiftly and effectively. For example, during II.v, set in the church, Annabella, carrying a microphone, entered during Giovanni's catalogue of her physical qualities and as the church setting was smoothly replaced by Florio's sitting room she sang 'Once I had a secret love'. Then, the scene change ended, with a banquet table now visible upstage, behind a gauze, Florio began II.vi, 'Where's Giovanni?'

The climax of the play was particularly effective (although the line of each character's thinking in V.v was not clear at all times;

see above, p. 113). Giovanni's gentle 'shhh' to his sister before finally stabbing her was a brilliant touch, as was letting us see him begin the final anatomy as the lights faded. The final scene was extraordinarily violent, with Giovanni completely soaked in blood (exactly as the text demands), Vasques returning with Annabella's body (rather than simply reporting the act), Donado trying to defend himself with a dinner knife, the Cardinal revealing himself as a coward, and spectacularly unpleasant deaths for Soranzo and Giovanni. What was particularly evident was how the careful construction throughout the production of both individual passions of love and hatred, and of a corrupt, malleable secular and religious society surrounding those individual desires, made explicable, indeed inevitable, the final explosion of violence, of which Annabella became, clearly, the sacrificial victim.

# 5　The Play on Screen

Compared with the extent to which Shakespeare's plays have been adapted to the cinema or television screen, the work of his contemporaries has been ignored in a similar fashion to the neglect it suffered for years on stage. Within this sparsely populated area, therefore, 'Tis Pity's three adaptations for the screen (in 1971, 1978 and 1980) make it one of the most filmed of early modern non-Shakespearean dramas. In addition, it also figured in Badger's Drift, the pilot episode of what became the long-running British television series Midsomer Murders. Throughout the episode, Cully, the aspiring actress daughter of the leading character, Detective Inspector Barnaby (played by the one-time Shakespearean actor John Nettles), is rehearsing for the part of Annabella, and a knowledge of the play's plot and characters (the first murder victim dies with the name 'Annabella' on her lips) helps tie up a loose end at the conclusion (see Wilkinson 2010: 55 for a full analysis).

## Addio, fratello crudele (Goodbye, Cruel Brother)
### dir. Giuseppe Patroni Griffi (1971)

The Italian director Giuseppe Patroni Griffi's film Addio, fratello crudele (Goodbye, Cruel Brother, with an English sub-title, 'Consumed by forbidden pleasure') was released in 1971, and is available on DVD with English sub-titles. The screenplay was 'freely adapted' from Ford's play, and focused almost entirely on two sets of relationships: one between Giovanni (Oliver Tobias), Annabella (Charlotte Rampling) and Soranzo (Fabio Testi), the other between Giovanni, Soranzo and the Friar (who are all, we learn from Soranzo, 'friends', though the friendship has not eroded the class difference between them). The characters of the Friar (played as a man much nearer

Giovanni's age than is common on stage) and Putana offer commentary on the action, while other roles such as Florio and Vasques are not named but simply referred to as 'Annabella's father' or 'Soranzo's manservant' and their roles are much reduced. Given the cutting, and the difficulty of translating Ford's poetic text to Italian, the screenplay is largely new, and the occasional repetition of lines taken directly from the play sometimes stand out rather startlingly. Watching the version dubbed into English (for all the actors apart from Tobias and Rampling) the text can seem mundane, though whether that is true of the effect of the Italian original I cannot say. Visually, however, the film (shot by cinematographer Vittorio Storaro) is stunning, and further enhanced by the lush, romantic orchestral score (by Ennio Moricone). The film is set in the Italian Renaissance, but to an even greater degree than the later British television version (see below), is removed from Ford's bustling Parma and set in a strangely idiosyncratic country house in a languid, wintry, bleak rural world. The plot follows Ford's to some extent but interpolates new scenes and events that are implied but not seen in the play. For example, trying to follow the Friar's injunction to overcome his desire for Annabella, Giovanni casts himself into a dried-up well, where, half-naked and to a background of forceful organ music, he endures the privations of hunger and cold, while the images of him seem by analogy to reflect Christ's struggle to overcome temptation in the desert, though his reasoning remains resolutely providential, that it is not his desire that drives him but his fate. Florio's house is located close to the Friar's monastery, and the monks work his land, closely intertwining the secular and religious forces in the play. The role of the Cardinal is transferred to a grim-faced abbot who underlines that the Church can absolve a sinner such as Annabella and show her compassion. But in return he expects and demands obedience and unqualified acceptance of his ruling that – in a reversal of responsibilities in the play – she should see her brother no more, a ruling the Friar delivers to the lovers before he leaves the monastery for ever.

The film stresses Giovanni and Annabella's shared family past, and their relationship does in fact remain fundamentally underpinned by the brother–sister bond. The scene of the sibling's 'betrothal' takes Ford's text literally. Picking up on their references to 'our mother's dust', Griffi puts the actors before a strange, candlelit setting of a tomb, exactly like those found in England in the seventeenth century, where the family of the deceased are carved kneeling, such as the memorial the widowed Duchess of Malfi refers to when, courting Antonio, she reminds him that she is not 'that figure, carved in alabaster, kneels at my husband's tomb'. Here, however, the figures are two-dimensional. Similar cut-outs, in wood, decorate the bed to which the siblings go to consummate their relationship, some replicating Renaissance–Classical motifs such as the three graces, alongside the image of the body of a woman in the pose of Botticelli's Venus, but with the head of an animal, perhaps inspired by the image of Leda and the Swan that Ford employs to underline the unnaturalness of this natural-seeming love scene (see p. 32). Here, however, Giovanni (unlike in the play) seems keen to downplay their sibling closeness: 'Don't call me brother, call me love.' This love scene (significantly in the light of the later bed-scene with Soranzo) is not explicit in any way: indeed they both remain swathed in their cloaks, and there is no specific representation of sexual love-making (though the blazing fire that warms them may suggest their passion). As they cautiously leave the chamber, Griffi inserts a short, silent moment where the children observe their father, Florio, bidding goodbye to a young woman with whom, clearly, he has just had sex.

The film is replete with undeniably arresting images, especially of containment and isolation. When Giovanni first encounters the Friar, Bonaventura is weaving an enclosure with ropes twined round posts, and Griffi's scene which combines Giovanni's awareness that Annabella must marry in II.i with the final moments of II.iv where Giovanni reveals his jealousy when Annabella shows him the jewel a suitor has given her (here a ring), is played with the two of them in a cage of birds, presumably to stress that their freedom, too, is constrained. Images of horses being trained or ridden seem to suggest how a powerful energy can be tamed; when the siblings ride through scores of white flags on poles, past a scaling-tower and battering ram and a trebuchet, before sitting on a catapult as Annabella comments that men die at war not of love, the symbolism of the setting underlines that it will be impossible for Annabella, besieged by the world around her, to avoid marriage and to remain true to Giovanni; and Lisa Hopkins outlines the pervading use of images of fires, windows and candles, and of 'the film's most sustained and striking visual patterning', that of imprisonment (2005: 67).

The film's second narrative focus is on the relationship between Annabella and Soranzo, which is, in some respects (made possible by the exclusion of other aspects of the play) filled out more than in Ford. Ford's III.ii is played (though shortened), and the marriage scene (also much shortened by the absence of Hippolita) cuts from Giovanni's refusal to drink the toast and Annabella's excuses for him (IV.i.26–8) to an interpolated scene in Annabella and Soranzo's bedroom, where a fire blazes as it did in the film's parallel love scene between the siblings. It is immediately clear that the relationship has not yet been consummated, but Soranzo (within the context of the mores of the time in which the film is set) is nevertheless restrained and understanding, denying he's angry, acknowledging she married him not because she loved him but because her father wanted her to, and expressing his willingness to be patient, in case she can come to love him. In a development not seen in the play, Annabella, removed from her father's to Soranzo's house, seems to be warming towards her husband. Riding together on the same horse, she seems relaxed with him, smiling, as they watch (the symbolism is a bit heavy here) two horses nuzzling each other before the stallion mounts the mare. Back at his home, Soranzo suggests the 'distraction' of a trip to Venice (perhaps prompted by the character's fondness in the play for Venetian poets). There, in a sexually very explicit, nude scene we see the couple make what looks like consensual love, after which they caress each other gently, she clearly enjoying the closeness of his body. Interestingly, however, the scene is partially shot at a 45 degree angle, which, to Hopkins, 'seems to suggest that it is this relationship which is exotic and strange, while what characterizes that between Giovanni and Annabella, initially at least, is precisely its normalcy and its grounding in the customary and familiar' (2000: 149). The portrayal of two lovers enjoying each other undoubtedly creates a particularly strong contrast with the mood when, Soranzo having appeared from their room, genuinely distressed, to call for a doctor, we next see him (with a return to Ford's IV.iii) abusing Annabella physically and violently, and threatening to kill her whole family (an echo of 'Knows thy old father this?', IV.iii.73), as he tries to bully the name of her lover out of her. With the Friar having exited the scene earlier, and without the tremendous scene in the play between Vasques and Putana (IV.iii.173–232), the film moves directly to V.v (with just a brief extract from V.iii). Here, the contrast between the

love scenes between Annabella and Giovanni and Annabella and
Soranzo becomes clear, making perfect sense of (the modernized
paraphrase of) Giovanni's opening lines asking whether Soranzo
has proved 'an expert husband, one much cleverer in devising night
games rather than innocent children as we were?' The through line of
the scene is rendered more straightforward than the emotional twists
and turns found in the play. Seemingly aware of and acquiescent to
her brother's plans, Annabella unbuttons her blouse to expose her
breasts, the lovers' bodies framed with the hilt of Giovanni's dagger
at a phallic angle towards her. As they did earlier, they both clasp the
dagger's hilt, and she pulls as much as he pushes the blade towards
her, saying 'Farewell. One more kiss my sister. [She kisses him.] I kill
you in a kiss', as she dies, and the music swells romantically as he
embraces her dead body, his lines then staying close to Giovanni's in
V.v.95 to the end of the scene.

The scene cuts to the banquet, a long table stretching the length of
a long room, with chairs down the side against the wall and a line of
candles opposite. Giovanni enters, naked to the waist and 'trimmed
with blood', with a very real-looking heart impaled on his dagger, but
(a mix of reality and symbolism) with red silk ribbons trailing from it.
He walks purposefully the length of the table to Soranzo, who stands.
Giovanni goes to stab him, but his arm is grabbed from behind by
Vasques, who holds Giovanni immobile. Soranzo takes the dagger
with the heart and stabs it into the table in front of Florio, takes
Florio's proffered dagger, calling for not one member of her family to
survive, so unleashing a bloodbath in which (in a scene reminiscent
of the St Bartholomew's Day massacre in Patrice Chereau's 1993 brilliant film *La Reine Margot*) Soranzo's men set about slaughtering all the
women present. In a series of intercut scenes we see Putana pursued
by Vasques; Giovanni stabbed with surgical precision in the heart by
Soranzo, pinning his body to a strangely carved wooden wall, the
camera lingering on his face as Soranzo watches him slowly die; the
mastiff we first saw with Annabella when her brother first confessed
his love for her runs along a corridor, sniffing at the dead bodies
strewn along it, before arriving at the body of Annabella, sprawled on
a bed at the top of blood-stained steps; the Friar trying to persuade an
implacable Soranzo – who wears a white leather collar, exactly like
the dog's – not to let Giovanni's dismembered body be cast into the
swamp. At that point a drum beat begins. A still shot of Giovanni's

bloodied head, in profile, cuts to the Friar leaving on horseback; then we see Putana being summarily beheaded by Vasques, watched by Soranzo wearing what looks like a wooden frame around his naked torso (trapping him like the spring-loaded chair that traps Ithocles in *The Broken Heart?*), before, behind the final credits, the image of a blood-red hill, capped by a tower, an image that suggests to Hopkins the inventive interpretation that 'as long as humans continue to be consumed by the fires of passion, the openness and emptiness of the landscape cannot prevent them from making prisons of their own' (2000: 150–1). The overall effect of the cutting (characters and plot lines) and emphases within the performances is to create a very different version of Ford's play from the one most likely to be gained by reading or seeing it on stage. But the excision of the sub-plot has at least the virtue of pointing up why it is so essential to the fabric of the play, and Roger Warren makes a good point in observing that setting the action so clearly in Renaissance Italy rather than Ford's English version of it 'made the business with the heart fit almost too well' and resulted in an 'insufficient clash between Giovanni's values and those of his society' (1988: 14).

In 1978 Belgische Radio en Televisie in association with Theater Arena Gent screened the play under the title *Toch Zonde dat 't een Hoer is*, directed by Dré Poppe and Jaak Van de Velde, with Ford's text translated into Dutch by Joël Hanssens. The cast included Hans Royards (Giovanni), Chris Thys (Annabella), Wim Huys (Soranzo) and Jo De Meyere (Vasques). I have been unable to trace and watch this version, but the completeness of the cast list available from the Internet Movie Database (IMDb) suggests that no particular plot-line or character was cut – not, at least, entirely – and that Bergetto and the Cardinal were the only roles played by a single actor.

## *'Tis Pity She's a Whore*, dir. Roland Joffé, BBC (1980)

Two years later, a version for television (only on VHS and very difficult to get hold of), directed by Roland Joffé, was broadcast on BBC2. Tim Pigott-Smith (who played Vasques) recalls that Joffé had been due to direct a film on the artist Stanley Spencer, which was pulled at the last minute by the BBC. *'Tis Pity* (which Joffé had directed for the National Theatre Touring Company in 1972) was substituted, with some of the cast of the Spencer project retained for the Ford. The characters for his stage production had been dressed in full Jacobean period costumes, with a flexible and indicative setting, appropriate to touring, of white drapes which could be manipulated to expose either 'the full width of the stage' or create 'antechambers and corridors' (Irving Wardle, *The Times*, 19 July 1972, quoted in Scott 1982: 102). The sibling lovers (Nicholas Clay and Anna Carteret) were presented as 'extremely young' and the production stressed 'the corruption of a society concerned only with money, authority and status, offset... by an intense realization of the couple's relationship' (Scott 1982: 102). For the televised version, however, Joffé transposed the play to a fully realized mid-nineteenth century setting, matched by a geographical shift from Italy to the north of England (if Florio's accent is a reliable guide), though it was actually filmed on location at Chastleton House, a Jacobean wool merchant's house, built between 1607–12 in Moreton-in-Marsh in the Cotswolds, an area of bucolic beauty in the west of England. The text was radically cut and rearranged and the cast list reduced and adapted: the role of Grimaldi was cut, along with the Banditti, and the Cardinal became the Lord Lieutenant (i.e. the monarch's local representative rather than the Pope's, and played magnificently by Alan Webb), so portraying a dominantly secular rather than religious society, with the Friar's role of implacable defender of faith becoming that of a pragmatic local vicar who knew that his best interests lay with Soranzo rather than God. The casting brought together an interesting mix of actors, some more associated with the classical theatre (Kenneth Cranham, Cherie Lunghi, Tim Pigott-Smith, Ron Pember, etc.) and others famous at the time for their television work in popular series (Bernard Archard in *Secret Army* and Rodney Bewes in *The Likely Lads*). It also created an age-range for the key male characters older than suggested by Ford's text. Anthony Bate's Soranzo, for example, presented Annabella (played here by Lunghi as an open, lively young woman whose affection for her brother appeared ordinary and optimistic) with the prospect of marrying a man twice her age rather than Ford's imagined 'gallant of three and twenty'. Her brother (clearly a neurotic in Cranham's brooding performance) was also, though to a lesser degree, some years older than her, which had the effect of further isolating Annabella rather than portraying the siblings as two young people united against the world around them. The Victorian milieu, however, was particularly appropriate for the underlying 'business' of finding Annabella a husband, and the emphasis on the house itself underlined the importance of 'property', whether real estate or a daughter or wife; the impressive wedding-cake for Annabella and Soranzo was in the shape of Florio's house. Putana's altered lines emphasized the priorities of this mercantile society where there is 'bargaining, talking, dealing on every side' rather than Ford's 'threatening, challenging, quarrelling and fighting' (I.ii.63–4). The setting of an isolated country house (though without the more extreme remoteness of setting in Griffi's film) removes the sense of the urban social context through which Annabella must pick her way, but creates a powerful sense of claustrophobia, where conversations are overheard, casual looks observed, and where we can easily understand Annabella's fear – accurate as it turns out – that 'The place is dangerous, and spies are busy' (V.i.54). The domestic scale of the house (there are few scenes set outside it) reflected the interior nature of Ford's fictional world and the intimate nature of his own theatre, allowing for scenes to be quietly spoken and for detailed inflections both vocally and physically, beneficial to scenes of secret love-making or persecution. The scene where Giovanni confesses to Annabella his love for her is played in what was once, clearly, their playroom. They sit, close together, right of screen, with the left-hand part of the screen dominated by a rocking-horse, a visual signifier of the relationship underlined by the frequent references to 'brother' and 'sister' in the dialogue. The powerful imagery of domestic life is used to particular effect in the scene between Vasques (Pigott-Smith playing him as a sadist with impeccable manners) and Putana (IV.iii) where he draws from her the name of Annabella's lover. They sit, two servants, below stairs, chatting and enjoying a cup of tea by a roaring fire. They are easy with each other, a slight crackle of sexual possibility in their looks and physical closeness. He tells her to remain seated while he gets boiling water to refresh the tea. Gently, he coaxes the lover's name out of her. As she reveals it he embraces her as if to kiss her, but instead reaches for the pot of boiling water and pours it over her face and eyes. He holds her while she screams. And, later, the vicar (and we) watch from an upstairs window as Putana, her scarring hidden by a scarf and bonnet, is dispatched from the house in a closed carriage.

The comic characters Bergetto and Poggio are particularly successful, partly due to the casting; Bewes (Bergetto) was, at the time the film was made, one of the most famous comic actors on television, while Pember (Poggio) was a vastly experienced actor able to play the foil to the idiot Bergetto in an understated way. With Grimaldi gone there could be no threat from him on Soranzo's life and therefore no mistaken murder of Bergetto in the dark. However, Richardetto and Philotis still remained, and the death of Bergetto (III.vii) and subsequent departure of Philotis to a nunnery (IV.ii) were rolled together in an interpolated scene where the couple eloped. Other elements were transposed to new scenes. For example, Hippolita's wedding masque and public death was cut, to be enacted in private by Vasques, who first engages in vigorous sexual intercourse with her before putting poison in a glass of wine, switching glasses and ensuring she drinks the poisoned one. Leaving her to die alone, painfully and slowly, Vasques brings Soranzo to see her body (Soranzo's evident difficulty in looking at it telling us in an instant why he was so dependent on his 'man'). The next shot is Vasques returning to Richardetto the small bag from which we had seen the manservant take the poison, a moment that echoes II.iii.57–60 where Richardetto promises to provide the toxin for Grimaldi's sword. Interestingly, however, there is no reference in this version to Richardetto being the still-living husband of Hippolita disguised as a doctor, leaving him simply to be, like the Friar, another man whose principles can be easily bought.

The most extensive interventions are made to the final act of the play, many designed to smooth out the various shifts in Ford's text that can (as the discussion on pp. 77–81 explores) present some difficulty in tracking the link between the characters' words and actions. Giovanni's soliloquy at the start of V.iii (in voice-over) is interrupted by the arrival of the Friar, delivering the letter from Annabella which (in a change from the original), we have already seen him show to Soranzo. This is followed (as in the play) by Vasques's invitation to Giovanni to attend Soranzo's birthday feast (though the telling and sharp exchange around Giovanni's use of the word 'dare' in his response is omitted). The Banditti are cut and the Cardinal is replaced by the Lord Lieutenant of the county, in line with the production's English and Protestant setting. V.iv opens with Giovanni arriving in Annabella's room, holding the letter which he uses to prompt his rebuke to his sister for her change of heart. The script stays close to Ford's text, though the reason for some cuts – such as Annabella's prophetic 'there's but a dining time / 'Twixt us and our confusion' – are to me difficult to understand. Overall, the scene is given a clean through-line. Annabella is much more committed to, and in control of what she clearly sees as their imminent deaths at Soranzo's bidding (if not precisely *his* hands) unless they take responsibility for their own end. On her line 'And be prepared to welcome it', she takes from under her pillow a case containing a cut-throat razor: her plan is clearly a mutual suicide pact. Giovanni, without her apparent belief in an after-life, is much less sure, but as in the play his doubts ('could', 'should') are challenged by her certainty ('certain', 'shall'). Her line 'Then I see your drift' is clearly played as her realization that the moment has come, and she prepares herself, willingly and lovingly giving him a kiss, and waiting as he gently caresses the vein he is about to sever. But this apparently consensual moment is only made possible by cutting those lines that complicate the scene. Out goes 'Will you be gone?', 'What means this?', and 'O brother, by thy hand', making the sequence one of a peaceful farewell to life on her part, with none of the dismay and fear that Ford's version weaves in. The last scene is played in Soranzo's dining room, the table set with a crisp white cloth, silver and crystal. Giovanni enters, not 'trimmed in reeking blood' as Ford imagined him, but dressed exactly as in the previous scene, and carrying a blood-stained napkin which he places on the table before Soranzo and which, on the line "You came to feast, my lords' (23), he opens to reveal his sister's heart. Florio expresses his horror and embarrassment (as in the play), but suffers no heart attack. The text is played reasonably complete up to Giovanni's line 'These hands have from her bosom ripped this heart' (59), at which point he is stabbed by Vasques and the guests sit in (presumably stunned) silence as he dies. In comparison with the climax to Griffi's film, the comparatively understated emotion in earlier moments and the deftly drawn domestic setting paid particular dividends here in showing the extremity of Giovanni's actions and their bizarre nature in this very English setting. Giovanni's death obviously makes the following text redundant and the scene cuts to l. 145, but introduces a new speech for the Lord Lieutenant to replace the Cardinal's: 'These deaths won't come to trial…' The final scenes are visual only. A group of men stand in the pouring rain at the burial of the siblings. Then we see Vasques (no banishment for him in this version) helping Florio into a carriage (an echo of the departure of Hippolita) leaving Soranzo and Vasques to turn towards the house which now, it appears, Soranzo owns. Florio's family and household have been erased.

# 6    Critical Assessments

Baldly stated, critical responses to 'Tis Pity for the past 400 years have returned time and time again to two linked issues: Ford's attitude to the incestuous relationship of Giovanni and Annabella – perceived by many to be at best ambivalent, at worst sympathetic – and the extent to which Giovanni can be considered a heroic figure or Annabella a victim. (There are, of course, notable exceptions to these preoccupations, especially the essays included in the collections edited by Anderson (1986), Neill (1988) and Hopkins (2010), and the book-length studies by Sargeaunt (1935), Oliver (1955), Leech (1957) and Stavig (1968) – though these rightly touch on those questions.) While it is true, as McCabe notes, that a 'tone of moral insecurity... pervades the entire text', it is equally important to recognize that incestuous love 'is its theme, not its platform' (1993: 229) and that its strength as a play derives precisely from Ford's refusal either to exonerate or condemn Annabella and Giovanni. However, critics have repeatedly confused sympathy with approval, so that until comparatively recently the word most often used to describe author and play has been 'decadent', which as Wymer notes, 'conveniently combine[s] moral and aesthetic implications' (1995: 87).

## Early responses

The debate around Ford's attitude to the incestuous lovers can be traced to the earliest surviving comments on 'Tis Pity made in a short, complimentary verse by Ford's friend Thomas Ellice, which was not included in some copies of the 1633 quarto edition but is included in most modern editions. Ellice, whose lines suggest he had seen the play rather than just read it, identifies as a *positive* quality Ford's balanced portrayal of Giovanni's and Annabella's actions and characters, allowing Giovanni's love to be 'unblamed' (4), and Annabella to remain 'Gloriously fair, even in her infamy' (10). Sixty years later, in his *Account of the English Dramatick Poets* (1691), Gerard Langbaine picked up the same tension but interpreted it as a major fault that lessens the play in comparison with others by Ford, and so set a critical trend that it would take centuries to dislodge: *'Tis Pity she's a whore* equals any of our author's plays; and were to be commended, did not the author paint the incestuous love between Giovanni and Annabella in too beautiful colours.'

With the play absent from the British stage, so far as we know, from the early 1660s until 1929 (see p. 106), and no text published between the 1633 quarto and Dodsley's in 1744, with another long gap before Gifford's edition in 1827, critical commentary remained scarce for two hundred years. It also remained largely unvaried and derivative. For example, in 1764, in *Biographica Dramatica*, David Erskine Baker drew directly on Langbaine in arguing that while the play could rightly be considered to be Ford's 'masterpiece', with many aspects of it being worthy of 'the immortal Shakespeare himself', its fatal weakness lay in its 'morals' (or rather lack of them), a flaw revealed in its unacceptably sympathetic portrayal of the lovers, especially Annabella who Ford had 'rendered... notwithstanding all her faults, so very lovely, that every auditor would naturally cry out to himself, "*'Tis Pity she's a whore*"'. Moreover, Baker adds, the 'catastrophe' of the play 'is too shocking for an audience to bear', however much they may keep telling themselves it is 'no more than a fiction' (1782 edition: 373–4).

Then, at the end of the eighteenth century, this anxious view of a delicate, if uneasy, balance of character and morality was bulldozed by Charles Dibdin in Volume III of his *A Complete History of the English Stage*: 'Nothing can be more revolting than the subject; and therefore, the warmer and more glowing the pictures of love are worked up, the more reprehensible is the author' (1797: 279). To Dibdin, playwrights had no business exploring deviant behaviour, let alone pleading or arguing for its acceptance. Their duty was to revile and censure it, especially incest which Dibdin argued has no place in the 'catalogue' of human behaviour 'without motive', though he does not suggest what that acceptable motive might be. But even he, again echoing Langbaine, admitted the literary abilities of the dramatist: 'all we can say of Ford is, to wish he had employed his beautiful writing to a more laudable purpose' (280).

## Nineteenth century: 'the sting of illicit passion'

The new century brought a fresh interest, tone and attitude to Elizabethan and Jacobean drama, stimulated by the publication in 1808 of Charles Lamb's enormously influential *Specimens of English Dramatic Poets who lived about the Time of Shakespeare*, a selection of 'scenes of passion, sometimes of the deepest quality, interesting situations, serious descriptions'. Lamb's censorious editorial stance ('I have expunged without ceremony all that which the writers had better never have written', p. xi) resulted in many of his extracts being brief and unrepresentative, and his book may have contributed to the (longstanding) notion that plays of the period tend to be a mix of good (to be praised and retained) and bad (to be regretted and cut). However, in the case of *'Tis Pity*, Lamb did at least try to hold together in suspension the two opposing dynamics of high-quality writing and by the choice and treatment of the subject matter:

> Ford was of the first order of poets. He sought for sublimity, not by parcels in metaphors or visible images, but directly where she has her full residence in the heart of man; in the actions and sufferings of the greatest minds.... Even in the poor perverted reason of Giovanni and Annabella... we discern traces of that fiery particle, which in the irregular starting from out of the road of beaten action, discovers something of a right line even in obliquity, and shows hints of an improveable greatness in the lowest descents and degradations of our nature. (1808: 217)

In very general terms, beyond a small core of works by Shakespeare, Jonson, Massinger and Fletcher, nineteenth-century attitudes to early modern plays as texts to read or plays to perform polarized between the Romantics – who saw the playwrights, in Edmund Gosse's words, as 'creators of sheet-lightning of poetry illuminating for an instant illuminating for an instant dark places of the soul' – and those who considered them as ramshackle hacks who occasionally turned out some sparkling verse but were generally unable to structure their work to meet either aesthetic criteria or to deal with subject matter that met with contemporary (or, in Ford's case, any) moral standards.

With the persisting dearth of stage productions by which their asser-
tions could be measured or challenged (see Chapter 4), critic after
critic – focusing on the extreme relationship between brother and
sister to the almost total exclusion of any consideration of the equally
important, but often mundane world that surrounds them – repeated
the same charge.

In 1811, William Gifford was in effect able to sum up the views of
nearly two hundred years of criticism when he wrote (in a review
of Henry Weber's 1811 edition of Ford's plays) that 'Tis Pity 'carries
with it insuperable obstacles to its appearance on a modern stage'
(*Quarterly Review*, December 1811: 466). Dismissing all efforts to see
any dramatic purpose in Ford's portrayal of the contrast between the
sibling lovers and the way of life of the Parman society surrounding
them, Gifford saw Giovanni *from his first appearance* as 'a professed
and daring infidel,... a shameless avower and justifier of his impure
purpose', with Annabella 'not a jot behind him in precocity of vice
[who]... had long suffered her thoughts to wander in the same
polluted path as her brother' (1895: xxxi–xxxii). He understood little
or nothing of early staging practices (confidently but uncomprehend-
ingly dismissing the stage direction at V.v as absurd, for example) and
often responded to characters in plays as if they were real people. At
the close of II.iii, for instance, he comments: 'What a detestable set
of characters has Ford here sharked-up for the exercise of his fine
talents! With the exception of poor Bergetto and his uncle, most of
the rest seem contending which of them shall prove worthiest of the
wheel and the gibbet.' Similarly, he considers Vasques an 'odious
wretch' and Annabella's responses to Soranzo in IV.iii to be 'perfectly
loathsome and detestable', though, tellingly, Soranzo himself escapes
any criticism. But even after all this Gifford, like those before him,
was forced to admire Ford's skill as a writer, though he still gives with
one hand while taking away with the other, suggesting that 'Its excel-
lencies far outweigh its defects' and suggesting that Ford's poetry
'flings a soft and soothing light over what in its natural state would
glare with salutary and repulsive horror' (1895: xliv).

Although stemming from a general dislike of Ford's work, it
comes as something of a relief from this 'great writer, pity about the
subject matter' criticism when William Hazlitt (in his *Lectures on the
Dramatic Literature of the Age of Elizabeth*, 1819, Lecture IV) casts a fresh
light on the issue, reversing the argument to claim that it was, in fact,

precisely 'the exceptionableness of the subject... which constitutes the chief merit of the play. The repulsiveness of the story is what gives it its critical interest' (1931: 268), while, apart from the 'simple painting and polished style' of some of the writing, he could find 'not much other power in the author... than that of playing with edged tools, and knowing the use of poisoned weapons' (1931: 268–9). Indeed, for Hazlitt, where Ford's plays in general 'have not the sting of illicit passion, they are quite pointless and seem painted on gauze, or spun of cobwebs' (1931: 269). Hartley Coleridge, who edited the plays of Ford and Massinger in 1840, found a kind of middle way, arguing in Ford's defence that although his plays were indeed based on 'horrible stories' it would be 'unfair from hence to conclude that he delighted in the contemplation of vice and misery', and that 'his genius was a telescope... powerful to bring within the sphere of vision, what nature has wisely placed at an unsociable distance' (1840: xlviii).

Matters remained pretty static until towards the end of the nineteenth century, when two critics weighed in with views that sought to challenge the judgements that had held sway, virtually unchanged, for nearly 250 years. In 1871, Algernon Swinburne, a firm advocate of the brilliance of Jacobean drama, wrote that he considered Ford to be 'a man worthy of note and admiring remembrance'. In defence of the fitness of the subject matter, Swinburne invoked a startling and provocative comparison with Ford's *Love's Sacrifice*, which 'is to me intolerable... it is utterly indecent, unseemly and unfit for handling. The conception is essentially foul because it is essentially false... The incestuous indulgence of Giovanni and Annabella is not improper for tragic treatment; the obscene abstinence of Fernando and Bianca is wholly improper' (1926: 382). The last major critical assessment of the nineteenth century was Havelock Ellis's New Mermaid edition of Ford's plays in 1888. In many respects, given Ford's interest in minds under stress, he and Ellis, a psychologist with a particular interest in all forms of sexual behaviour, were well matched. In his Introduction, Ellis, who considered Ford 'the most modern of the tribe to whom he belonged' (1960: xv), commented that all his work offers a picture of the 'conflict between the world's opinion and the heart's desire' (xiv). Ellis, however, does not use the word 'incest', but refers to Ford 'presenting an image so simple, passionate, and complete, so free comparatively from mixture of weak or base elements, as that of the boy and girl lovers who were brother and sister' (xii). Indeed, this evasiveness and special pleading continues in terms perhaps more applicable to the film *Blue Lagoon* than the tragedy of two young, but fully responsible, young adults: 'When we think of Ford we think of Giovanni and Annabella, passionate children who have given the world for love; of the childish sophistry with which they justified themselves' (xv). Ellis presumably sought by this tactic to divert critics of the play's immorality; to our modern perceptions he may have achieved quite the opposite.

## Ford and decadence

Tempting as it might be to see these views of the amorality of *'Tis Pity* as exemplary of Victorian sensibilities, and to expect a more open response in the twentieth, the views of both play and playwright as morally deficient have continued. S. P. Sherman set the ball rolling with his 1908 essay 'Ford's Contribution to the Decadence of the Drama', arguing that while *'Tis Pity* 'represents the height of Ford's achievement as a dramatist', it also revealed 'the depth of his corruption as an apostle of passion... bent on laying bare... a ferocious and ugly story of almost unmentionable lust and crime'. The cause of this, according to Sherman, was 'the unmistakable savour of decadence in his work [which] delights kindred souls, but sorely offends the Conservative' and which undoubtedly 'had its influence in closing the theatres in 1642' (xvii). The result was to create a view of Ford (and other Caroline dramatists, views now dismissed by most critics) as decadent writers both morally and artistically, repeating tired conventions from the vibrant earlier period, driven to stage ever greater excesses in order to satisfy the jaded palates of a sated Cavalier audience and so ultimately responsible for Parliament's order for the closure of the playhouses in 1642. Even William Archer, a critic who took the early modern dramatists very seriously, described Ford in *The Old Drama and the New* as a dramatist of the 'abnormal' (1923: 63), and just two years later, Allardyce Nicoll, an extremely influential figure, wrote in *British Drama* that in *'Tis Pity*

> we are thoroughly immersed in the world of romantic decadence. [Ford's] love of dismal incident and nauseous sexual relationships mark him out as the product of an age of degeneracy... decadence of thought is all that

can explain… the terrible scene at the opening of the second act, in which Giovanni, with all the callousness of a degenerate age, informs Annabella she must marry… [If] an audience pitied Annabella, they could only do so out of their own diseased imaginations…. The novelties in the torments… have no dramatic purpose; they are there merely to arouse curiosity and thrill [sic] in the hearts of a jaded public. (1925: 191–3)

By 1926, with the view of Ford as a decadent dramatist firmly established, and with most critics continuing to describe Ford as an apologist for incest, others started to examine the play from different perspectives beyond merely asserting that the writer was a moral defective. In his Introduction to the 1933 Everyman edition of *Webster and Ford: Selected Plays*, for example, G.B. Harrison explained that Ford 'suffered that complete loss of moral indigna- tion which often comes from much study of psychology' (though Harrison offers no evidence to support this questionable gener- alization), as a consequence of which, 'Abnormal passions excited in Ford, not repugnance, but curiosity' (xii). Two years later, in her influential study *Themes and Conventions of Elizabethan Tragedy*, Muriel Bradbrook helped set this view of Ford as a writer unable to control his material, arguing not on points of morality, but his abilities as a writer:

> [Ford's] decadence may be summed up as an attrition rather than a coars- ening. His faults arise from gawkiness, an attempt to deal with subjects outside his limited range. This does not prevent him from producing some work which is, in a minor way, quite flawless…. Yet his relationship to the writers of the great period is that of an imitator. He took over conventions passively and therefore they were largely useless to him. Moreover, the attrition represented by *'Tis Pity She's a Whore* is serious. The Elizabethan drama had worked itself out in Ford. (1935: 260–1)

## Mid-twentieth-century responses

In 1932, T.S. Eliot published Selected *Essays 1917–1932*, which included his essay on Ford, written in the book's year of publication. When the essay was reprinted in *Elizabethan Dramatists* (1963), Eliot wrote patronizingly in the Preface that whereas 'for the understanding of Shakespeare, a lifetime is not too long', it may be that 'a youthful sensibility [Eliot was 44 when he wrote his essay on Ford, around the age Ford was when he wrote the play] is the most desirable qualification for writing about these minor poets and dramatists' (1963: 6). Consequently, Eliot reverted to the tiresome 'comparison with Shakespeare' gambit in his attempt to place his dramatists on a scale of achievement. He is generally dismissive of Ford, considering that he 'had no conception of what [Shakespeare] was trying to do', speaking a 'cruder language' and writing 'drama of the surface'. Of the 'use of incest' in *'Tis Pity* – 'Ford's most famous, though not necessarily best, play' – Eliot considered that there 'should be no objection of principle', but argued that the test of the play is whether Ford can 'give universal significance to a perversion of nature which… is defended by no one' (124). Eliot praised Ford (if faintly) for not trying to 'make the unpleasant appear pleasant', for the occasional 'fine' verse (he cites Annabella's lines, V.v.16–29), and for the fact that the 'low comedy, bad as it is', is both more restrained and relevant to the plot than he finds in Ford generally; indeed, he considers the death of Bergetto 'almost pathetic'. He saves his most severe criticism for the characterization of the lovers (Giovanni 'almost a monster of egotism', Annabella 'virtually a moral defective', and he finds (in another, inevitable, comparison with Shakespeare) the lack of a sense of an 'overpowering attraction' such as in *Antony and Cleopatra*, merely a 'carnal infatuation'. Eliot had, I suspect from this, not *seen* the play (he makes no mention of the Phoenix Society's 1923 production, the only one he could have witnessed), and that, added to his insistence on calling Ford a 'poet' rather than a playwright, may account for his superficial observations.

Despite Fredson Bowers' sane reminder that critics should not 'mistake for the dramatist's own statement of the moral, the arguments of a character in a fevered state of emotion' (1940: 211) some continued to worry away at the question of whether Ford was too uncritical of his protagonists, others moved to shift the blame for this lapse from Ford's own weakness to the demands of an audience, so creating the image of a writer 'effectively mugged by his own characters', and leaving us with the notion of Ford as a writer who, had he had his own way, 'would have had his characters spend all their time at tea-parties' (Hopkins 2010: 25). In 1961, R.J. Kaufmann's essay 'Ford's Tragic Perspective' took a new line, arguing that Ford's thinking was essentially in line with that of contemporary French philosophy, and that 'The Sartre of *The Flies* would recognise a brother in the Ford of *'Tis Pity'*, with its portrayal of Giovanni as a man who '"calls" himself to a role that his residual nature... will not permit him to fulfil', and for whom the only solution is the nihilistic one of a 'powerful and personally organized death' (1961: 358). Kaufmann initiated other responses focusing on Ford's 'modernity', relating him to existentialists and Artaud's Theatre of Cruelty in particular.

## Ford's four hundredth anniversary

In 1986, the four hundredth anniversary of Ford's birth provided an opportunity to reflect on the state of Ford studies. Donald K. Anderson's collection *'Concord in Discord': The Plays of John Ford, 1586–1986* (1986) included a number of essays that took a fresh look at long-standing aspects of Ford criticism, with Richard Ide's on Ford's 'Belatedness' (see p. 91), Alan Dessen's on what scholars can learn from stage productions and Mark Stavig's return to the question of the play's condemnation of Giovanni. Two years later, reviewing current Ford criticism in the Introduction to *John Ford: Critical Re-Visions* (1988), Michael Neill identified the ongoing obsession with Ford's 'decadence' and 'moral obliquity', and the absence of a modern edition of his work. Neill's volume sought to open up new avenues of enquiry (or new to Ford studies), with essays grouped around the broad areas of formalist, new historical, intertextual and performance approaches. Three essays in particular opened up new lines of enquiry: Neill's on the emblematic power of Ford's stage imagery; Verna Foster's (developing ideas first expressed by Margot Heinemann) that saw the play as sitting somewhere between *Romeo and Juliet* and Middleon's city comedies; and Martin Butler's argument (focused on *The Broken Heart* but directly applicable to *'Tis Pity*) that Ford's quotation of other dramatists' work reflected a self-conscious, witty theatricality shared by Inns of Court dramatists (though I depart from Butler's view in that I think such quotations are designed to guide responses to the play rather than simply make the audience feel clever).

## Structure and tone

Before Ben Jonson asserted himself as a *writer* of plays, the common term for a dramatist was a play*maker*, a term which reminds us that the structure of a play, the way its component parts are put together, is a key aspect of the playwright's craft. Although *'Tis Pity*'s themes and moral standpoint have dominated critical discussion, the way Ford orders his plays has also attracted interest. T.S. Eliot's dismissal of the Hippolita subplot, for example, as 'tedious' and 'superfluous' is typical of a number of critical responses, though others, if not always favourably, have addressed themselves more carefully to how Ford makes his play. Thelma N. Greenfield, for example, believes that Ford did not share the same 'susceptibility to narrated event' of Webster or Shakespeare, but that his 'creativity and drive were sparked by a response to stage-worthy scenes and dramatically ambiguous questions' (1986: 15). To the last point there can be no disagreement, but Greenfield's comments might be construed as suggesting that *'Tis Pity* merely moves from one startling event to another. More nuanced is Sargeaunt's observation that Ford 'knows how to begin a play... he knows how to fill up the gaps in his audience's knowledge of events that happen off the stage during the play' and that, as a result, he 'demands of the audience that they shall fill in the gaps between the scenes'. However, she is more critical of what she sees as his clumsy use of sub-plots and, in particular, the comic characters within them:

> In *'Tis Pity She's a Whore* the presence of the low comedy scenes is more unfortunate than in any other of Ford's plays. For... their intrusion into a play with such a theme is at times almost unbearable, and the play in itself, apart from such blemishes, is, with the possible exception of *The Broken Heart*, unequalled by any other work of Ford's. (1966: 92)

She is not alone, and the critical viewpoint expressed in this quotation, with its use of words like 'low comedy', 'intrusion' and 'blemishes' reflects a longstanding difficulty critics and to some extent audiences have found with the shifts in mood and tone of Jacobean tragedies in general, and with *'Tis Pity* in particular. Even Ford himself seems to have been in two minds about mixing comedy and serious drama. In the Prologue to *The Broken Heart* he declared that his audience should have no expectations:

> Of apish laughter, or of some lame jeer
> At place or persons; no pretended clause
> Of jests fit for a brothel courts applause
> From vulgar admiration. (4–7)

Such fripperies would not, he implies, be appropriate for the austere Spartan setting of the play, and, in similar vein, he reassures the spectators of his history play *Perkin Warbeck* that it contains no "Unnecessary mirth forced, to endear / A multitude' (Prologue, 23–4). The presence of laughter in the most serious plays, is, of course, virtually a defining characteristic of early modern drama (White 1998: Chapter 6 *passim*), and in that respect, it is these two plays that look more out of line than *'Tis Pity* in terms of contemporary dramaturgy. It is also true, however, that this particular aspect of the plays can present performers and, to a greater extent, critics with problems, though the impact of this mix can really only be fully assessed by seeing rather than just reading the plays, so dependent is it on the presence of the actor. For example, critical responses to the comic sub-plot surrounding Bergetto and Poggio have generally been unfavourable, even among his admirers. In 1932, the entry in *The Cambridge History of English Literature*, after trotting out the same old charge of immorality, went on to assert that

> in his attempts at comedy, Ford sinks to a lower level than any dramatist of his class, and his farce lacks much of the coarse buffoonery of his predecessors. It is not realistic; it is not the expression of high spirits; it is a perfunctory attempt to season tragedy and romance with an admixture of rubbish, without humour and without joy. (196)

This frankly lazy piece of criticism, much of the 'comic relief' school of understanding the role of comic and serious action set against, or mingled with each other, was however repeated by critics who one might expect to know better, especially once the play began once more to have at least some life in performance. For example, the otherwise acute Ronald Huebert argues that Putana's joke about Annabella having 'passed under' rather than over 'a paradise of joy' (II.i.39–41), that the line is 'hardly funny at all in any accepted sense of that word', and 'could not possibly raise more than a wry and uncomfortable smile' (1977: 85). Huebert nowhere in his book refers to any performances of the play, but my own experience as a director and audience member does not support his view (and the video recording of the 1991 RSC production will bear me out). In fact, Ford's comic writing generally comes in for some tough criticism, much of which my own contact with the plays simply does not bear out.

Ford's sub-plots are seen by some critics as especially weak. In her influential study of Jacobean drama, Una Ellis-Fermor described them as 'utterly incongruous… concessions to the needs of the theatre rather than a spontaneous expression of his thought. They have, in fact, no valid part in the main business of his plays' (1965: 227), while Sargeaunt remarks that 'Ford's futile attempts at comedy merely disgust one by the unseemly irrelevance of their buffoonery' (1966: 153):

> The weakest part in the construction of Ford's plays is not in his treatment of the central theme, but in the presence of extraneous matters, sub-plots, incidents and characters structurally unrelated to the main plot. This unrelated material is of two kinds; it is either melodrama or low comedy. (Sargeaunt 1966: 71)

While I don't for a moment underestimate the difficulty that a modern audience can have with seventeenth-century jokes I could hardly disagree more strongly with these judgements (and I have tried to address the issue directly in my discussion of I.iii in Chapter 2 and with reference to stage and screen productions in Chapters 4 and 5). So far as the Bergetto sub-plot is concerned, the fact that the character appears in six of the 16 scenes up to and including III.vii would suggest that Ford considered the role a significant one, and his death marks a tipping point in the play.

However, an even more challenging matter – and an aspect of especially Jacobean drama invoked in discussions of its 'decadence' – is the laughter that often accompanies the scenes of bloodletting with which early modern tragedies frequently conclude, and the climactic scene of 'Tis Pity may well produce this response in its audience. In his study of revenge tragedies (with which 'Tis Pity has some affinities) John Kerrigan distinguishes between comic scenes and those moments in revenge plays when 'vengeance generates... a strain of awkward comedy which raises laughter and kills it' (1997: 216). The most dangerous example of this in *'Tis Pity* is the moment when Giovanni appears with the heart on his dagger. According to Michael Neill, 'No adequate account of Ford's dramaturgy could avoid coming to terms with this scene' and unsurprisingly its scrutiny has led to a wide range of responses to what for 'audiences and readers alike... is the most shocking, eloquent and unforgettable of all the play's stage pictures' (Neill, 1988: 155). Indeed, I would set it alongside images of Hamlet with the skull, Titania embracing Bottom as an ass and the conspirators standing over Caesar's body as iconic visual moments in early modern drama. It is an image that can be said to define the stage violence so closely associated with Jacobean tragedies of blood, and to encapsulate the complex of audience expectations and response such violence stimulates. Nicholas Brooke neatly identifies the 'conjunction in this shock of horror, emotional satisfaction, and derisive laughter [as] a brilliant but difficult climax' that presents problems in staging. But his suggestion that if instead of a 'sheep's heart dripping real blood... a large cardboard heart is used, the symbolic point is clear but the shocking actuality is lost' is less convincing, as the point is that this is not a symbol, but the real thing. Brooke claims that the cardboard solution 'is sometimes done' (Brooke 1979: 124), but I have found no record of this in any professional production. In trying to explain why 'the play's intelligence requires' that response, Brooke argues that the 'laughter depends on the aesthetic perfection which the laughter must attack' and that the play 'rests on an aesthetic of tragedy which is at once beautiful and ridiculous', asserting that while 'the play's laughter is not so wildly disturbing as Tourneur's or Webster's, nor as morally serious as Middleton's... it is still essential, for the play centres on an intellectual idea of tragedy that is perceived as at once beautiful and absurd' (1979: 125, 127). My own view is that this 'horrid laughter' is best understood through the concept of the grotesque. The impact of the grotesque identified by the Roman writer Vitruvius in the visual arts is equally applicable to drama: a sense of confusion in the viewer caused by the presence of incompatible elements and responses. It was, in effect, 'a style in which renaissance artists could express some of the tensions that arose from the incompatibility between the ideals espoused and imposed by government, by church, by university, by all the agencies of institutional culture, and the actualities of individual experience' (Hauser 1965: 138). The nineteenth-century writer and artist John Ruskin captures the mood of a scene such as V.vi, I think, when he writes of those Renaissance artists who employed the strategies of the grotesque that 'it is because the dreadfulness of the universe around him weighs upon his heart that his work is wild', and, however disturbing, we should embrace the fact that Ford may be actively demanding laughter at this climactic moment as part of the shifting and disturbing ambiguities that lie at the very heart of his play.

## Language and style

In 1819, Thomas Campbell, considering what to incorporate in his *Specimens of the British Poets*, declined to include any extracts from 'Tis Pity on the grounds that 'Better that poetry should cease, than have to do with such subjects'. As I noted earlier, however, generally even the harshest critics have acknowledged the skill of the writing. Gifford, for example, asserted that Ford's poetry 'flings a soft and soothing light over what, in its natural state, would glare with salutary and repulsive horror' (1827: Vol. II, p. xxiv; Gifford's is, as Kathleen McLuskie rightly observes, by implicitly separating language and character, an 'unthe-atrical reading' of the play, but it does signal a 'tension in Ford's work between characters who are capable of poetic insights and those to whom it is denied', 1981: 209). Swinburne was perhaps the first critic to pay *detailed* attention to Ford's dramatic verse, likening its impact on him it 'to a mountain lake shut in by solitary highlands, without visible outlet or inlet, seen fitlier by starlight than sunlight... steel-blue and sombre, with a strange attraction for the swimmer in its cold smooth reticence and breathless calm' (1925–7: 372). (T.S. Eliot admired some of Swinburne's critical judgements, preferring them to Lamb's, but was less keen on his prose style.) He then moved to an analysis of *how* Ford created this effect:

> Nothing is more noticeable in this poet than the passionless reason and equable tone of style with which in his greatest works he treats of the

deepest and most fiery passions, the quiet eye with which he searches out the darkest issues of emotion, the quiet hand with which he notes them down. At all times his verse is even and regular, accurate and composed; never specially flexible or melodious, always admirable for precision, vigour, and purity. (1925–7: 372)

As an example of this verse style in action Swinburne quoted the exchanges between Annabella and Giovanni in V.v.26–37:

In a few words that startle as with a blow and lighten as with a flame, the naked natural spirit is revealed, bare to the roots of life. And this power Ford also has shown here at least; witness the passionate subtlety and truth of this passage, the deepest and keenest of his writing, as when taken with the context it will assuredly appear. (1925–7: 375)

For William Archer, Ford, like Webster, 'cultivated a fashion of abrupt utterance, whereby an immensity of spiritual significance – generally tragic – was supposed to be concentrated into a few brief words' (1912: 297). Muriel Bradbrook, quoting V.iii.11–15, observed that the 'contrast between the strength of feeling and the quietness of the statement is something new' in contemporary drama, where 'the tone depends on the lack of rhetoric', and noting the significance of Ford's use of endearments as 'one of the ways of heightening the horror' argued that it 'works by hints, not statements' (1935: 251–3). Her assertion that Ford 'is quite unable to manage quarrels or debates' (255) cannot hold up under an analysis of the scenes with the Friar, or IV.i or IV.iii., and here Bradbrook misses the power not only of Ford's ability to embody Annabella's 'sincere directness' by employing both the 'extraordinary simplicity and directness of expression' that characterizes his writing at its 'highest level', with rhetoric that carries Giovanni's 'boastful utterance' (Sargeaunt 1966: 158), as well as failing to recognize the relationship between language and action such as in the final two scenes of the play. Indeed, as I have pointed out in the Commentary, Ford (like the best of his contemporaries) is able to use complex blends of forms of verse and prose, and to add to that spoken language, sound and silence, and striking visual images, often enhanced by music, that together create the world of the characters, and our experience of and insight to the passions of minds and moralities under pressure.

## Contemporary criticism

An important contribution to Ford studies since Neill's in 1988 is
the collection edited by Lisa Hopkins (2010). In it, at the opening of
her survey of recent criticism of 'Tis Pity, Sandra Clark quotes Mario
DiGangi's view that 'Ford scholarship has not kept pace with the
upsurge in Renaissance dramatic scholarship since the 1980s' (2010:
60). It is true that some critics continue to harp on about whether
or not Ford is too sympathetic in his treatment of the incestuous
lovers, and Carla Dente (1999) attempted (unsuccessfully in my
view) to resurrect the image of Ford as a decadent writer, but others
(including the contributors to Hopkins' volume) have thankfully
moved on to explore new topics or revisit established ones with fresh
eyes. Particular areas of current interest include the investigation
of the social/political dynamics the play rests upon or challenges,
such as in Bruce Boehrer's *Monarchy and Incest in Renaissance England*
(1992) that sees the play as critical of Stuart absolutism, ideas that
are also addressed by Molly Smith (1998), Julie Sanders (2006), Lisa
Hopkins and others. Related to these studies are those that examine
the author's and the play's relationship to Catholicism (Clerico 1992,
Hopkins) and to the established Protestantism of Ford's time. A
consequence of the shift towards the domestic, the social and the
private in many contemporary plays was an increased emphasis on
the role of women, and studies such as Nathaniel Strout's terrific
1990 essay, Marion Lomax's introduction to her edition (1995), Alison
Findlay's *A Feminist Perspective on Renaissance Drama* (1999) and Judith
Haber's *Desire and Dramatic Form in Early Modern England* (2009) have
broadened understanding of the sexual politics in 'Tis Pity. Some
critics – Luis-Martinez (2002), Hopkins, Smith (1998) – have looked
at the play's languages, verbal and physical, from new perspectives,
while 'Tis Pity has also benefitted from the general exploration of the
cultural context of early modern drama and the move away from
Shakespeare as the central site of discussion of the plays in performance in their own time, an offshoot of this being an awareness of the
links between playhouses and anatomy theatres.

    Finally, a number of recent critics have looked at the core issue of
incest from different perspectives. For example, Richard Marienstras
(1985) explored Elizabethan attitudes to incest in terms of its challenge

to patriarchy, seeing Giovanni's incest as 'a means of killing the father' (195); in 1993 Richard McCabe asserted that 'Sexuality is political as politics is sexual, and incest functions as an appropriate metaphor for political disturbance' (120); and Molly Smith developed these ideas further, reading the play as an example of 'theatre's appropriation of religious vocabulary to depict the most serious of social trangressions, incest', with incest seen 'as a threat to sociocultural boundary formation' in which Ford daringly and consciously usurped 'the vocabulary of devotional literature to represent a relationship that flagrantly violates all social and moral codes.... By violently yoking the sacred and transgressive, *'Tis Pity* thus proffers a more radical reassessment of Renaissance ideologies than any other play of its time' (1998: 12, 116). More recently, Judith Haber has returned to Marienstras's argument but developed it to see the incest as having a 'double-edged force' with the play's ending insisting both on the 'breaking of paternal law – embodied in the breaking of Florio's heart – and its fulfillment' (2009: 110).

# Further Reading

## Editions

The text and all line references in this book are taken from Martin Wiggins (ed.)*'Tis Pity She's a Whore*, New Mermaids (London: A&C Black, 2nd edition, 2003), and checked against the Scolar Press Facsimile of the 1633 edition held in the Bodleian Library, University of Oxford. Other editions consulted include:

Barker, Simon (ed.) (1997) *'Tis Pity She's a Whore*, London: Routledge.

Coleridge, Hartley (1840) *The Dramatic Works of Massinger and Ford*, 2 vols, London: Edward Moxon.

Ellis, Havelock (ed.) (1888) *The Best Plays of John Ford*, Mermaid series, London: Yizetelly & Co. Re-issued in 1960 as *John Ford (Five Plays)*, London: Ernest Benn.

Gifford, William (ed.) (1827) *The Dramatic Works of John Ford*, 2 vols, vol. 1, London.

Gifford, William (ed.) (1895) *The Works of John Ford, with Notes by William Gifford, Esq., carefully Revised by the Rev. Alexander Dyce*, 3 vols, vol. 1 (originally published 1869) London: Lawrence & Bullen, .

Lomax, Marion (ed.) (1995) *John Ford: 'Tis Pity She's a Whore and Other Plays*, Oxford: Oxford University Press.

Massai, Sonia (ed.) (2011) *'Tis Pity She's a Whore*, London: Arden Shakespeare.

Roper, Derek (ed.) (1975) *'Tis Pity She's a Whore*, The Revels Plays, London: Methuen.

The Revels Student Edition (1997), also edited by Roper, prints the 1975 text but includes a new Introduction that takes a different view of a number of aspects of the play.

Sturgess, Keith (1970) *John Ford: Three Plays*, Harmondsworth: Penguin Books.

## Further Reading

Abate, Corinne S. (2010) 'New Directions: Identifying the Real Whore of Parma' in Lisa Hopkins (ed.) *'Tis Pity She's a Whore: A Critical Guide*, London: Continuum, pp. 94–113.

Amtower, Laurel (1988) "'This Idol Thou Ador'st": The Iconography of '*Tis Pity She's a Whore*', *Papers on Language and Literature*, 34: 2, 197–206.

Anderson Jr, Donald K. (1972) *John Ford*, Twayne's English Authors Series, New York: Twayne.

Anderson Jr, Donald K. (1962) 'The Heart and the Banquet: Imagery in Ford's '*Tis Pity* and *The Broken Heart*', *Studies in English Literature, 1500–1900* 2: 2, 209–17.

Anderson Jr, Donald K. (ed.) (1986) *Concord in Discord*, New York: AMS Press.

Archer, William (1912) *Play-Making: A Manual of Craftsmanship*, London: Chapman & Hall.

Archer, William (1923) *The Old Drama and the New*, London: Heinemann.

Archibald, Elizabeth (2002) "'Worse Than Bogery":' in Elizabeth Barnes (ed.) *Incest and the Literary Imagination*, Gainseville: University Press of Florida, pp. 17–38.

Artaud, Antonin (1968, 1971) *Collected Works*, vols 1 and 2, trans. Victor Corti, London: Calder & Boyars.

Artaud, Antonin (1970) *The Theatre and Its Double*, trans. Victor Corti, London: Calder & Boyars.

Baker, David Erskine (1782) *Biographica Dramatica, or, A Companion to the Play-House*, 2 vols, London.

Barnes, Elizabeth (ed.) (2002) *Incest and the Literary Imagination*, Gainseville: University Press of Florida.

Bergeron, David M. (1986) 'Brother–Sister Relationships' in Donald K. Anderson Jr (ed.) *Concord in Discord*, New York: AMS Press, pp. 195–219.

Billing, Christian (2004) 'Modelling the Anatomy Theatre and the Indoor Hall Theatre: Dissection on the Stages of Early Modern London', *Early Modern Literary Studies*, Special Issue 13: 3 (April), 1–17: http://purl.oclc.org/emls/si-13/billing

Boehrer, Bruce (1992) *Monarchy and Incest in Renaissance England*, Philadelphia, PA: University of Pennsylvania Press.

Bowers, Fredson (1940) *Elizabethan Revenge Tragedy*, Princeton, NJ: Princeton University Press.

Bradbrook, Muriel (1935) *Themes and Conventions of Elizabethan Tragedy*, Cambridge: Cambridge University Press.

Brooke, Nicholas (1979) *Horrid Laughter in Jacobean Tragedy*, London: Open Books.

Bueler, Lois E. (1980) 'Role-Splitting and Reintegration: The Tested Woman Plot in Ford', *Studies in English Literature, 1500–1900* 20: 2, 325–44.

Bulman, James (1990) 'Caroline Drama' in A. R. Braunmuller and Michael Hattaway (eds) *The Cambridge Companion to English Renaissance Drama*, Cambridge: Cambridge University Press, pp. 353–79.

Butler, Martin (1984) *Theatre and Crisis, 1632–1642*, Cambridge: Cambridge University Press.

Butler, Martin (1988) '*Love's Sacrifice*: Ford's Metatheatrical Tragedy' in Michael Neill (ed.) *John Ford: Critical Re-Visions*, Cambridge: Cambridge University Press, pp. 201–231.

Campbell, Thomas (1845) *Specimens of the British Poets*, London: John Murray.

Cartelli, Thomas (1991) *Marlowe, Shakespeare, and the Economy of Theatrical Experience*, Philadelphia: University of Pennsylvania Press.

Carter, Angela (1995) 'John Ford's '*Tis Pity She's a Whore*' in *Burning Your Boats: The Collected Short Stories*, London: Chatto & Windus.

Champion, Larry S. (1975) 'Ford's '*Tis Pity She's a Whore* and the Jacobean Tragic Perspective', *Publications of the Modern Language Association of America* 90, 78–87.

Clare, Janet (2006) *Revenge Tragedies of the Renaissance*, Tavistock: Northcote House.

Clerico, Terri (1992) 'The Politics of Blood: John Ford's '*Tis Pity She's a Whore*', *English Literary Renaissance* 22: 3, 405–34.

Davril, Robert (1954) *Le Drame de John Ford*, Paris: Librairie Marcel Didier.

Dawson, Lesel (2008) *Lovesickness and Gender in Early Modern English Literature*, Oxford: Oxford University Press

Dente, Carla (1999) 'Reading Symptoms of Decadence in Ford's '*Tis Pity She's a Whore*' in Michael St John (ed.) *Romancing Decay: Ideas of Decadence in European Culture*, Aldershot: Ashgate, pp. 27–38.

Dessen, Alan C. (1985) *Elizabethan Stage Conventions and Modern Interpreters*, Cambridge: Cambridge University Press.

Dessen, Alan C. (1986) ''*Tis Pity She's a Whore*: Modern Productions and the Scholar' in Donald K. Anderson Jr (ed.) *Concord in Discord*, New York: AMS Press, pp. 87–108.

Dessen, Alan C. and Thomson, Leslie (1999) *A Dictionary of Stage Directions in English Drama, 1580–1642*, Cambridge: Cambridge University Press.

Dibdin, Charles (1797–1800) *A Complete History of the English Stage*, 5 vols, London: printed for the author.

Eliot, T. S. (1963) *Elizabethan Dramatists*, London: Faber & Faber.

Ellis-Fermor, Una (1965 [1936]) *The Jacobean Drama: An Interpretation* (5th edition), London: Methuen.

Farr, Dorothy M. (1979) *John Ford and the Caroline Theatre*, Basingstoke: Macmillan.

Fehrenbach, R. J. (1986) 'Typographical Variation in Ford's Texts: Accidentals or Substantives?' in Donald K. Anderson Jr (ed.) *Concord in Discord*, New York: AMS Press, pp. 265–94.

Findlay, Alison (1999) *A Feminist Perspective on Renaissance Drama*, Oxford: Blackwell.

Forker, Charles R. (1990) *Fancy's Images: Contexts, Settings, and Perspectives in Shakespeare and His Contemporaries*, Carbondale and Edwardsville, Ill: Southern Illinois University Press.

Foster, Verna (1988) "'Tis Pity She's a Whore as City Tragedy' in Michael Neill (ed.) *John Ford: Critical Re-Visions*, Cambridge: Cambridge University Press, pp. 181–200.

Frost, David L. (1968) *The School of Shakespeare: The Influence of Shakespeare on English Drama 1600–42*, Cambridge: Cambridge University Press.

Greenfield, Thelma N. (1986) 'John Ford's Tragedy: The Challenge of Re-Engagement' in Donald K. Anderson Jr (ed.) *Concord in Discord*, New York: AMS Press. pp. 1–26.

Haber, Judith (2009) *Desire and Dramatic Form in Early Modern England*, Cambridge: Cambridge University Press; especially Chapter 8, '"Old men's tales": Legacies of the Father in *'Tis Pity She's a Whore*'.

Hauser, Arnold (1965) *Mannerism*, London: Routledge & Kegan Paul.

Hazlitt, William (1931) *Lectures on the Dramatic Literature of the Age of Elizabeth*, number iv, in P. P. Howe (ed.) *Complete Works of William Hazlitt*, vol. 6, London: J.M. Dent and Sons, Ltd., pp. 268–9.

Heilman, Robert B. (1986) 'The Perverse: An Aspect of Ford's Art' in Donald K. Anderson Jr (ed.) *Concord in Discord*, New York: AMS Press, pp. 27–48.

Heinemann, Margot (1980) *Puritanism & Theatre: Thomas Middleton and Opposition Drama under the Early Stuarts*, Cambridge: Cambridge University Press.

Hogan, A. P. (1977) "'Tis Pity She's a Whore: The Overall Design', *Studies in English Literature, 1500–1900* 17: 2, 303–16.

Homan Jr, Sidney J. (1967) 'Shakespeare and Dekker as Keys to Ford's *'Tis Pity She's a Whore*', *Studies in English Literature, 1500–1900* 7, 269–76.

Hopkins, Lisa (1994) *John Ford's Political Theatre*, Manchester: Manchester University Press.

Hopkins, Lisa (2002) 'Incest and Class: *'Tis Pity She's a Whore* and the Borgias' in Elizabeth Barnes (ed.) *Incest and the Literary Imagination*, Gainseville: University Press of Florida, pp. 94–113.

Hopkins, Lisa (2005) *Screening the Gothic*, Austin, TX: University of Texas Press.

Hopkins, Lisa (ed.) (2010)*'Tis Pity She's a Whore: A Critical Guide*, London: Continuum.

Houlahan, Mark (2010) 'New Directions: The Deconstructing *'Tis Pity*?: Derrida, Barthes and Ford' in Lisa Hopkins (ed.) *'Tis Pity She's a Whore: A Critical Guide*, London: Continuum, pp. 136–51.

Howe, P. P. (ed.) (1931) *The Complete Works of William Hazlitt*, 21 vols, vol 6, London: J.M.Dent & Sons.

Hoy, Cyrus (1960) '"Ignorance in Knowledge": Marlowe's Faustus and Ford's Giovanni', *Modern Philology* 57, 145–54.

Huebert, Ronald (1977) *John Ford, Baroque English Dramatist*, Montreal and London: McGill-Queen's University Press.

Ide, Richard (1986) 'Ford's *'Tis Pity She's a Whore* and the Benefits of Belatedness' in Donald K. Anderson Jr (ed.) *Concord in Discord*, New York: AMS Press. pp. 61–86.

Kaufmann, R. J. (1961) 'Ford's Tragic Perspective' in R. J. Kaufmann (ed.) *Elizabethan Drama: Modern Essays in Criticism*, Oxford: Oxford University Press, pp. 356–72.

Kerrigan, John (1997) *Revenge Tragedy*, Oxford: Clarendon Press.

King, T. J. (1964–5) 'The Staging of Plays at the Phoenix in Drury Lane, 1617–42', *Theatre Notebook* 19, 46–66.

King, T. J. (1992) 'Thomas Nabbes's *Covent Garden* (1638) and Inigo Jones's Drawings for the Phoenix or Cockpit in Drury Lane' in John H. Astington (ed.) *The Development of Shakespeare's Theater*, New York: AMS Press, pp. 185–202.

Lamb, Charles (1808) *Specimens of the English Dramatic Poets who Lived about the Time of Shakespeare*, London: Edward Moxon.

Langbaine, Gerard (1691) *An Account of the English Dramatick Poets*, Oxford: L.L. George West and Henry Clements.

Leech, Clifford (1957) *John Ford and the Drama of His Time*, London: Chatto & Windus.

Leggatt, Alexander (1988) *English Drama: Shakespeare to the Restoration, 1590–1660*, London: Longman.

Lever, J. W. (1971) *The Tragedy of State: A Study of Jacobean Drama*, London: Methuen.

Lomax, Marion (1987) *Stage Images and Traditions: Shakespeare to Ford*, Cambridge: Cambridge University Press.

Luis-Martinez, Zenon (2002) *In Words and Deeds: The Spectacle of Incest in English Renaissance Tragedy*, Amsterdam: Costerus New Series 145, Editions Rodopi B. V.

Marienstras, Richard (1985) *New Perspectives on the Shakespearian World*, trans. Janet Lloyd, Cambridge: Cambridge University Press.

McCabe, Richard (1993) *Incest, Drama and Nature's Law, 1550–1700*, Cambridge: Cambridge University Press.

McGuiness, Patrick (2000) *Maurice Maeterlinck and the Making of Modern Theatre*, Oxford: Oxford University Press.

McLuskie, Kathleen (1981) 'John Ford' in Philip Edwards, G. E. Bentley, Kathleen McLuskie and Lois Potter (eds) *The Revels History of Drama in English*, vol. IV 1613–1660, London and New York: Methuen, pp. 202–10.

McLuskie, Kathleen (1986) '"Language and Matter with a Fit of Mirth": Dramatic Construction in the Plays of John Ford' in Michael Neill (ed.) *John Ford: Critical Re-Visions*, Cambridge: Cambridge University Press, pp. 97–127.

Meads, Chris (2001) *Banquets Set Forth: Banqueting in English Renaissance Drama*, Manchester: Manchester University Press.

Moore, Antony (ed.) (2002) *Love's* Sacrifice, Manchester: Manchester University Press.

Neill, Michael (ed.) (1988) *John Ford: Critical Re-Visions*, Cambridge: Cambridge University Press.

Neill, Michael (1988) '"What Strange Riddle's This?": Deciphering *'Tis Pity She's a Whore'* in *John Ford: Critical Re-Visions*, Cambridge: Cambridge University Press, pp. 153–74.

Nicoll, Allardyce (1925) *British Drama: An Historical Survey from the Beginnings to the Present Time*, London: Harrap.

Norbrook, David, and H.R. Woudhuysen (1992) *The Penguin Book of Renaissance Verse, 1509–1659*, London: Penguin Press.

Oliver, H. J. (1955) *The Problem of John Ford*, Melbourne: Melbourne University Press

Sanders, Julie (2006) *Adaptation and Appropriation*, London: Routledge.

Sargeaunt, Joan M. (1966) *John Ford*, New York: Russell & Russell. First published Oxford: Blackwell, 1935,

Sawday, Jonathan (1995) *The Body Emblazoned: Dissection and the Human Body in Renaissance Culture*, London: Routledge.

Scott, Michael (1982) *Renaissance Drama and a Modern Audience*, Basingstoke: Macmillan.

Sensabaugh, G. F. (1944) *The Tragic Muse of John Ford*, Stanford: Stanford University Press.

Sherman, S. P. (1908) 'Ford's Contribution to the Decadence of the Drama' in W. Bang (ed.) *John Fordes Dramatische Werke*, Louvain: A. Uystpruyst.

Silverstone, Catherine (2010) 'New Directions: Fatal Attraction: Desire, Anatomy and Death in *'Tis Pity She's a Whore'* in Lisa Hopkins (ed.)*'Tis Pity She's a Whore: A Critical Guide*, London: Continuum, pp. 77–93.

Smallwood, R. L. (1981) *''Tis Pity She's a Whore* and *Romeo and Juliet'*, *Cahiers Élisabéthains* 20: 49–70.

Smith, Molly (1998).*Breaking Boundaries: Politics and Play in the Drama of Shakespeare and His Contemporaries*, Aldershot: Ashgate.

Stavig, Mark (1968) *John Ford and the Traditional Moral Order*, Madison: University of Wisconsin Press.

Stavig, Mark (1986) 'Shakespearean and Jacobean Patterns in *'Tis Pity She's a Whore'* in Donald K. Anderson Jr (ed.) *Concord in Discord*, New York: AMS Press, pp. 221–40.

Stone, Lawrence (1965) *The Crisis of the Aristocracy*, Oxford: Oxford University Press.

Strout, Nathaniel (1990) 'The Tragedy of Annabella in *'Tis Pity She's a Whore'* in D. G. Allen and R. A. White (eds) *Traditions and Innovations*, Newark, DE: University of Delaware Press, pp. 163–76.

Swinburne, Algernon (1926) *The Complete Works of Swinburne*, 20 vols, vol XII, (ed.) Sir Edmund Gosse and T. J. Wise, London: Heinemann, 371–406.

Traub, Valerie (1992) *Desire and Anxiety: Circulations of Sexuality in Shakespearean Drama*, London: Routledge.

Ure, Peter (ed.) (1968) *The Chronicle History of Perkin Warbeck: A Strange Truth*, London: Methuen.

Ward, A. W. W. (ed.) (1932) *The Cambridge History of English Literature*, Vol. VI, Cambridge: Cambridge University Press.

Warren, Roger (1988) 'Ford in Performance' in Michael Neill (ed.) *John Ford: Critical Re-Visions*, Cambridge: Cambridge University Press, pp. 11–27.

White, Martin (1998) *Renaissance Drama in Action*, London and New York: Routledge.

White, Martin (2009) *The Chamber of Demonstrations: Reconstructing the Jacobean Indoor Playhouse*, Bristol: Ignition Films for the University of Bristol.

Wilkinson, Kate (2010) 'The Performance History' in Lisa Hopkins (ed.) *'Tis Pity She's a Whore: A Critical Guide*, London: Continuum, pp. 34–59.

Williamson, Audrey (1951) *Theatre of Two Decades*, London: Rockliff.

Wiseman, Susan J. (1990) *''Tis Pity She's a Whore*: Representing the Incestuous Body' in Lucy Gent and Nigel Llewellyn (eds) *Renaissance Bodies*, London: Reaktion Books, pp. 180–197. Reprinted in Stevie Simkin (ed.) (2001) *Revenge Tragedy*, Basingstoke: Macmillan, pp. 208–28.

Wolfit, Donald (1954) *First Interval: The Autobiography of Donald Wolfit*, London: Odhams Press.

Woods, Gillian (2010) 'New Directions: The Confessional Identities of *'Tis Pity She's a Whore*' in Lisa Hopkins (ed.) *'Tis Pity She's a Whore: A Critical Guide*, London: Continuum, pp. 114–35.

Wymer, Roland (1986) *Suicide and Despair in the Jacobean Drama*, Brighton: Harvester,

Wymer, Roland (1995) *Webster and Ford*, Basingstoke: Macmillan.

Wymer, Roland (2002) '"The Audience is Only Interested in Sex and Violence": Teaching the Renaissance on Film' in *Working Papers on the Web*, 4 (September): www.shu.ac.uk/wpw/renaissance/wymer.htm

# Index